HERMANN KUHN

THE KEY

TO THE

CENTER

OF THE

UNIVERSE

CROSSWIND PUBLISHING
Germany: 31505 Wunstorf • P.O.Box 2210 • Tel: (0)5033 - 911 040
USA: P.O.Box 3312 • Incline Village • NV 89450

Die Deutsche Bibliothek - CIP-Einheitsaufnahme

Kuhn, Hermann:
The Key to the Center of the Universe
/ Hermann Kuhn. Wunstorf : Crosswind Publ., 2001
ISBN 3-9806211-8-9

Published previously as:
'The Notion of Growth'

We are interested in your comments.
You can contact us at

Crosswind Publishing

USA: P.O.Box 3312
           Incline Village
           Nevada, NV 89450
           Fax: 775 - 831 9527
           email: cwpubl@aol.com

Germany: P.O. Box 2210
           31505 Wunstorf
           Fax: 01149 - (0)5033 - 911 045
           email: crosswind@t-online.de

Front Cover Photo: Wolfgang Götte

This book is dedicated to

SRI ARYANANDI MUNI MAHARAJ

in deep gratitude.

परस्परोपग्रहो जीवानाम्

'The purpose of souls is to assist each other.'
TATTVARTHASUTRA – Chapter 5, Sutra 21

CONTENTS

Fascination

Everyone starts life with enthusiasm. With each step we venture into our new world we discover things unknown we explore with fascination, delight and wonder.

This fascination accompanies our early years. It reaches an absolute high when we fall in love for the first time and to our amazement discover _within us_ an unexplored, dormant world of fantastic feelings, - a world whose existence we couldn't even have guessed at before and that now promises unfathomable ecstatic joy. This discovery inspires us to try out entirely new action-patterns and make us venture into utterly unknown areas of our life.

After this first ecstatic high our fascination usually diminishes. Inevitable disappointments cause us to be more cautious especially in the area of our emotions, so that deep pain may not overwhelm us too easily. Yet instead of searching how to renew the original enthusiasm that guided us so playfully in our early years, we now restrict everything that could fill our life with liveliness again.

More or less willingly we accept the advice whispered by our environment (school, relatives, friends etc.) that now the seriousness of life would start and that the rest of our days will conform to a solemn pattern of reduced happiness. We learn to value our enthusiasm less than material and emotional stability - though in the long run all such stability either proves highly fleeting and built on quicksand, or solidifies life into a death-like state where nothing is able to move us any more.

In all this we follow the overwhelming example of our fellow people. With hardly any resistance we accept a life only occasionally inspired by fascination and enthusiasm, but that for the most part grinds us down in increasingly monotonous and dull routine.

Yet no matter how soothing this illusory stability appeals to us most of the time, it violently tears us apart when sometimes out of the blue we become aware how deeply we locked ourselves into desolate confining boundaries. We sense that this cannot possibly be everything, that life should offer more than stagnant resignation and ever diminishing real happiness. An almost irrational yearning for breaking loose, for carefree excitement, for daring adventure rises within us - the yearning for the very type of fascination that made us experience our youth so vividly.

If we detest to continue life in this unfulfilled longing, with these relentless, desperate bouts of disappointment, then we _have_ to fundamentally alter our present situation, then we _have_ to search for other worlds we can explore with the same enthusiasm that infused our youth with so much liveliness. If our present world becomes too narrow, too limited for us, then we need to find new ideals, values, objectives _beyond these limits_ so that the fascination and intensity of our early life will rouse again.

THE KEY TO THE CENTER OF THE UNIVERSE describes how to discover a new, hidden world within us that becomes the more fascinating the deeper we venture into it. It is the path to the center of our consciousness that never was described in such clarity and practicability in our times. The path is independent of any philosophical orientation or faith and open to everyone without restriction.

It is a path to experience the majesty, the grandeur, the infinite breadth of our being everyone senses within - if he is only courageous enough to admit this notion.

The knowledge of this path was handed down from times beyond history. It tells us how to disentangle ourselves from undesired events. It describes immense, untapped abilities inborn in all of us, and tell us how to unfold their power far more efficiently than we presently do.

Aim of this path is _not_ the annihilation of our individuality in some faceless enlightenment, nirvana, satori or brahman, or insight into how this world truly works. The main aim of this path is _not_ found on the level of our mind. The main aim is an ever growing comprehensive, _loving_ understanding, - a compassionate expansion of our being that unfolds more with every single step, yet never violates or extinguishes our individuality. With loving understanding our insights leave the cold level of intellect and mind and gain unmatched vivaciousness and depth.

Once we discover that deep within us, beyond all our familiar perceptions, there exists a hidden, fantastic world that - when unlocked - introduces us to ecstatic dimensions of love, happiness, energy and unprecedented clarity of insight, our original vibrant fascination with life resurges again. The state we then enter equals the exciting discovery of our first falling in love, yet its kaleidoscopic vivaciousness far transcends everything experienced previously.

Once we know the entrance to this world, fascination never leaves us again. To experience this we only need to activate abilities dormant within us all. Our consciousness then unfolds with the same easiness with which we grew from a newborn baby into our present form.

The Ancient Wisdom How to Unfold Life

THE KEY TO THE CENTER OF THE UNIVERSE presents the first chapter of an Indian manuscript of great antiquity - the Tattvarthasutra. The

Tattvarthasutra describes in concentrated form one of the oldest, if not the oldest philosophy of the world.

The work introduces an refreshingly new, unconventional view of purpose and functioning of our consciousness that far surpasses all Western, matter-oriented concepts. It identifies the mechanisms that make us really _EXPERIENCE_ this world. It alerts us to channels through which to perceive and access it we are unaware of. It hands us a radically alternative model - a second opinion - of our universe that does _not_ see us as _separate_ from it, but as its very _center_, - just as we experience it in everyday life. It allows us to see life _not_ as an infinite mass of disjointed events we feel unconnected to, but empowers us to steer every event that concerns us in an innovative, highly effective way.

Far from being a theoretical treatise, the work accompanies its advice with easily applicable, practical methods how to systematically access higher dimensions of our life.

The knowledge is part of the Jaina Canon that is customarily counted as one of the major religions of the world. Yet in essence this label is wrong. In contrast to many other philosophies, religions and ideologies the Tattvarthasutra has no intention to teach mankind respect before real or imaginary (one or many) gods, nor to pray in any form for divine blessing. It also does not want to convert all and everyone into blind-believing devotees to let their lives revolve around some luminous spiritual magnet.

The Tattvarthasutra describes nothing other than a method, an instrument how to unfold hidden abilities of exceptional magnitude we all carry within. These abilities open up such breathtaking depth and broadness of knowledge, love, energy and the experience of happiness Western culture has no concept to match.

The Tattvarthasutra contains a practical key that systematically expands our understanding and triggers experiences of superior states of consciousness. This key is not shrouded in obscure language nor does it demand the application of mystic techniques, _it simply interprets life from a new angle_. Yet this new angle enables us to arrange the components of our daily life in such a way that our consciousness automatically shifts into new modes of operation.

This method leads to total independence. It unfolds abilities generally attributed only to supernatural beings. We achieve this not by fickle divine sanction or by surrendering to a guru. The method of the Tattvarthasutra causes - only in step with our own efforts - the gradual dissolution of obstructions that limit our consciousness. In growing self-determination we then recognize our own personal path with ever increasing clarity. The Tattvarthasutra describes exactly how this is achieved.

The Tattvarthasutra

The Tattvarthasutra is about 1800 years old. Its title translates '*The Text Describing the Purpose of Reality*'.

It was written in the second or third century AD by the Indian sage Umaswami, who condensed the vast contemporary knowledge of this path in this one work.

Yet the knowledge of the Tattvarthasutra is based on still older wisdom. It origins reach far beyond recorded history. There exists evidence of 24 enlightened teachers who taught identical knowledge at much earlier times. Corresponding artifacts have been found in the Indus Valley Culture, the oldest Asian civilization (approx. 3000 BC and before) and the records mentioned in other manuscripts reach even further back. The Tattvarthasutra is regarded as the main work on this path.

'Sutras' (short statements) and their interpretation through commentaries originated in times when paper and other means of material recording did not exist. Knowledge was learned by heart and handed down orally from generation to generation. Sutras therefore were kept as brief as possible. They were governed by precise rules which for example defined the weight of a word by its position alone. To keep knowledge pure, even the commentators followed exact rules. This method worked with such precision that highly complex information conceived thousands of years ago reached our present times with hardly any distortion.

To someone raised in a Western cultural environment, the transfer of knowledge by brief sutras may appear strange and unfamiliar at first. Complex rules and formal style can easily block access to these works, - especially when translated in dry scholarly fashion that does not convey the ingeniousness, inspiration and power of the original sutras.[1]

Yet though the outer form of this millennia-old work looks unusual, it has not lost any of its original fascination, impact and practicality. A growing number of people searching for _purpose beyond material saturation_ recognize it as their main key to unknown dimensions of their existence. - The new frontier of human experience lies _within us_. - The Tattvarthasutra outlines exactly how to explore these uncharted dimensions.

The Tattvarthasutra covers three major themes:

Part 1 - chapter 1 - introduces the sheer magnitude of our potential. It explains how this universe supports the physical expression of all the ideals, desires, ideas and aspirations we carry deep within us. It describes through what channels we gain access to knowledge of higher order and how to intuitively discriminate between truth and error. It reveals how to experience higher dimensions of our consciousness.

Part 2 - chapter 2 to 5 - outlines the levels of existence on which life manifests. This part also deals with the purpose and functions of time, space, matter and other basic elements of this universe.

---

[1] Unfortunately most scholars attempting an interpretation lack the direct personal experience that is essential if one wants to bring the spirit of this ancient work to life. Familiarity with Sanskrit grammar alone just does not automatically produce understanding of the fascinating higher dimensions of consciousness the sutras describe. It also does not automatically bestow the ability to translate this work into a language easily understood by those in search of this information.

Part 3 - chapter 6 to 9 alerts us to the factors that limit our present state of life and explains how to remove their causes. Chapter 10 describes our shift into a state where we are free from all limiting influences and can access the entire breadth and richness of our potential.

THE KEY TO THE CENTER OF THE UNIVERSE presents the first part of this ancient manuscript. It introduces the magnitude of our potential and tells us how to explore it in our daily life.

The third part of the Tattvarthasutra has been published as KARMA - THE MECHANISM by Hermann Kuhn (also at Crosswind Publishing). It alerts us to deep-rooted, hidden mechanisms that govern all our actions and tells us how to control them. The work contains all parts of the Tattvarthasutra that explain the _karmic mechanisms_ relevant to our present times (chapter 6, 8, and part of chapter 9). Special efforts have been made to present the _practical_ aspect of the Tattvarthasutra - the mechanisms of action and the development of hidden abilities - in an easily applicable way.

A modern commentary accompanies the ancient text. For easier reading all accents in the transliteration of Sanskrit words have been eliminated. The Sanskrit terms are for reference only. They help to identify the exact meaning.

How to Use This Book

It is recommended to read the book twice and to defer all questions that might arise during the first reading. The text often introduces themes only briefly to return to them extensively later. A second reading then produces far deeper insight.

It is further recommended to try to locate the described mechanisms _in our own_ life rather than to ponder how they might effect _others_, what others may think about them, or how much _they_ would be able to understand. As long as we remain on this level of 'mere theoretical' understanding and avoid _actively testing_ the mechanisms in _our own_ life, the ancient manuscript will not reveal its hidden power.

'TEXT OF THE SUTRAS' lists the text of the ancient manuscript without accompanying commentary.

'APPLICATION' - the second part of the book - offers further information how to make practical use of this knowledge. This information is derived from other parts of the Tattvarthasutra, further ancient scriptures and practical experience.

SUTRAS

THE KEY

TO THE

CENTER

OF THE

UNIVERSE

Chapter 1 of the
- Tattvarthasutra -

SUTRA 1

सम्यग्दर्शनज्ञानचारित्राणि मोक्षमार्गः ॥ १ ॥

Samyag darshana jnana charitrani moksha margah (1)

- The intuition how to optimally unfold our consciousness (*samyag darshana*)
- knowledge that makes us recognize and understand this unfolding of consciousness (*samyag jnana*) and
- the manifestation of these insights in action (*samyag charitra*)

are the path to liberation. (1)

Three factors need to act together to enable the dynamic unfoldment of our consciousness that makes us perceive new, more comprehensive and far more fascinating dimensions of life:

1 - <u>The intuition how to optimally unfold our consciousness</u> (*samyag darshana*) is the ability to spontaneously choose from the innumerable alternatives of daily life the *one optimal* action that makes us perceive and experience vast, unknown and far more fascinating dimensions of life.

This intuitive ability to find our path to inner growth is no mystic faculty that needs to be trained tediously through esoteric techniques, but nothing other than a special feature of our perception called *darshana* in Sanskrit.

darshana is intuitive comprehension; - it is the emotional weight we assign to sense-impressions and insights. By intuitive comprehension we select from all the possible actions of daily life the one we feel most attracted to.

Our intellect plays hardly any role in this process. It is far too slow to compute in advance all the consequences our actions may have in the fast pace of daily life.

Yet we also know that our intuition may easily lead us astray and cause undesired results.

This book therefore describes a <u>special feature</u> of intuitive comprehension <u>that excludes error and flawed understanding</u>. The Sanskrit term for this special feature is '*samyag darshana*'; in this book it is called <u>'Orientation towards Growth'</u>.

Intuitive orientation towards growth is a natural, inherent ability of our consciousness, which everyone can unfold. The author of the Tattvarthasutra demonstratively positions this ability at the very start of his work and thereby emphasizes its central importance for our development.

Orientation towards growth is like a red line that leads from our present situation directly to the highest dimensions of our consciousness. It enables us to spontaneously and with unerring assuredness select only those actions that propel us towards ever widening perception and towards realizing the immense abilities dormant within us. It allows us to intuitively identify flawed information and exclude them from our path.

Intuitive orientation towards growth is the essential key for a type of expansion that leads to freedom from all restricting influences. Its development and application is the guiding theme of all the topics of this book.

Yet this feature of *samyag darshana* (orientation towards growth) is only the practical expression of this far more comprehensive term. The entire scope and depth of *samyag darshana* is revealed in the second sutra.

Sutra 3 describes how to develop our intuitive orientation towards growth and how to expand its range.

Sutra 15 explains how to use this type of intuition to access hidden parts of our reality.

2 - <u>Knowledge that makes us recognize and understand this unfolding of consciousness</u> (*samyag jnana*) opens our awareness for the mechanisms that make our hidden abilities become real.

We generally assume that if we want to explore new areas of experience, we first need to acquire knowledge and then to apply it. Yet reality works exactly the opposite way. We *first* experience something new and *then only* begin to search - more or less intuitively and often subconsciously - for concepts that may explain our new experiences and connect them to our current understanding. This process is especially true for all expansion of consciousness that makes us perceive areas *beyond* our familiar sphere of life.

Contrary to common belief most experiences of expansion of consciousness are hardly ever clear and vivid enough to make us recognize them the very moment they happen. Most insights into different (new) levels of consciousness are so brief that they appear like highly fleeting, almost unreal apparitions. Since we mostly cannot explain what we experienced, we usually store these events in the same place as all the other unresolved experiences that accompany our life and which we choose to ignore or forget as well.

Hidden deep inside our memory we therefore carry a number of experiences we are barely aware of, but which nevertheless contain vital information how higher, more advanced states of existence feel like.

The type of knowledge mentioned in the sutra (*samyag jnana*) has the purpose to alert us to these hidden experiences and to make them accessible.

It is special knowledge that can reach us through a variety of channels. Some of these channels are unknown to the West or their mechanisms are misunderstood. Sutras 9 - 31 explain the bandwidth and range of each of these channels, the different types of knowledge they transmit and how we can use them.

It is not of primary importance whether this special knowledge reaches us through verbal instruction, by reading respective descriptions or by sudden intuitive comprehension.

The knowledge awakens us to _that_ part of the path _we already experienced_ - that is its main feature.

If we already have access to superior levels of experience without knowing it, this knowledge (_samyag darshana_) makes us aware of this opening. For this to happen we need to acquaint us with the characteristics of the more advanced states of consciousness and then link these characteristics to our special insights.

It always pays to take interest in this special knowledge because it enlivens areas of our consciousness we are unfamiliar with, but that nevertheless exist.

Yet it is impossible to expand our consciousness _by study alone or by mere intellectual understanding_.

Simultaneously with every insight into the higher functions of our consciousness we also receive the ability to fully comprehend our experience. This happens automatically., no matter if we are aware of it at the moment of insight or not. Experience and understanding are just two different aspects of the same event.

Misinterpretation, prejudice, ignorance, doubt and social consensus usually prevent us from understanding and utilizing these expansive experiences. Yet when we allow our intuitive orientation towards growth (_samyag darshana_) to guide this process, these obstructive factors are automatically filtered out. This kind of flawless intuitive insight makes us intuitively sense how every information we receive will influence our progress. It gives us the choice to accept and amplify only those impulses that positively lead us to more advanced stages of development.

3 - **Manifesting our insights in action** (_samyag charitra_) means to really _do_ what will free our consciousness and action from all restrictions. The transfer of our insights into action is essential if we truly want to experience superior dimensions of our consciousness.

Many who strive for an expansion of consciousness believe that this should happen on a purely mental ('spiritual') level and therefore must be accompanied by some withdrawal from worldly activities. They usually maintain the idea that the more comprehensive the withdrawal, the faster their spiritual progress will be.

Convictions of this type often cause disdain for physical activities and the instrument of this activity - our body - while at the same time all mental (spiritual) efforts assume a disproportionately high significance. In this frame of mind all action (and even the body itself) may be rejected as annoying, troublesome, obstructive and interfering with spiritual growth.

The sutra makes clear that _activity_ is an inalienable factor in our growth. Only when we transfer our insights into action will we be able to access the more advanced dimensions of our consciousness. Any exclusively mental ('spiritual') occupation with esoteric contents - irrespective of how intensely and seriously we go about it - neglects one of the three essential factors of growth and is therefore unable to produce the optimal and stable unfolding of our consciousness.

Activity is an essential part of our life in the state of embodiment. Through activity we strive for fulfillment (realization) of the values and ideals we feel deep within ourselves. The emotional engagement with which we pursue these values acts like a magnet that attracts all components necessary for their fulfillment.

This emotional engagement allows us to experience the themes of our life until we gained optimal insight from them and our emotional attachment to the completed themes falls off.

Yet our emotional bond to _unfinished_ themes of life continues to remain active _even if we reject_ their transfer into activity. Without manifesting them in activity our life will continue to revolve around these unfinished themes - whether we like it or not - and thereby prevent us from experiencing superior, far broader dimensions.

When we seriously begin to direct our activities towards inner growth, we rapidly become able to arrange our actions so intelligently that unwanted themes of life either fall away or are completed in their shortest possible time.[1] Insights into superior levels of consciousness will then rise automatically.

Freedom from all limiting influences (*moksa*) is a state where all our hidden abilities are fully realized. These abilities, which all of us always carry within us, open such breathtaking breadth and depth of comprehension, love, power and the experience of and capacity for happiness, Western culture has no concept to match. We reach this ultimate freedom when we remove all elements that block the unrestricted operation of our consciousness. Once these blocks are fundamentally gone, we automatically gain access to this highest status of our life.

The Tattvarthasutra offers us a method to realize this highest status. It contains a practical key that systematically opens hidden dimensions of our consciousness. This key is not shrouded in obscure language or requires the exercise of mystic techniques, *it simply interprets life from a new angle*. Yet this new angle enables us to arrange the components of our daily life in such a way that more expansive insights will rise automatically.

When we put this method into practice, we enter a path to total self-determination and to the attainment of abilities generally attributed to supernatural beings only. Yet we reach this state not by fickle divine sanction, the attendance to mystic powers or through surrender to a guru. The method of the Tattvarthasutra causes - in step

---

1 The chapter 'FIVE FREEDOMS' introduces the main factors that assist this process. KARMA - THE MECHANISM (also by Hermann Kuhn) explains the practical application of this knowledge in daily life.

with our own efforts - the gradual dissolution of obstructions that limit our consciousness.

The sutra mentions three factors. Yet this does not mean that each factor constitutes a path all by itself. *Only the combined application of all three factors*:

- the *intuition* how to optimally unfold higher insight and experience within us

- our *conscious understanding* of the mechanisms that produce this unfolding of consciousness and

- *using* the abilities and insights gained this way *in action*

will give us access to dormant levels of our consciousness that far exceed all Western imagination.

S U T R A   2

तत्त्वार्थश्रद्धानं सम्यग्दर्शनम् ॥ २ ॥

Tattvarthashraddhanam samyagdarshanam (2)

Confidence in the purpose of reality is the origin of our intuitive orientation towards growth (*samyag darshana*). (2)

The striving for fulfillment (manifestation, realization) of all the values and ideas we feel deep inside us is a fundamental characteristic of our existence.

Reality enables us to express all these ideas, ideals, values and concepts. Reality is a growth-process in which our inner striving for these values becomes physical experience.

One of the essential characteristics of this process is to always break up static situations that restrict our growth[2]. This mechanism

---

2 and also to stall actions that are detrimental to our development

prompts us to become open to ever new experiences and to unfold an ever growing understanding of reality.

It is _not_ the main purpose of our reality to give permanence to material components that may accompany our actions, but to stimulate us to always seek out _new_ fields of experience. Whatever - positive or negative - circumstances we find ourselves in always lose their importance for our life as soon as we gained optimal insight from them. When this happens, they cease to engage our interest and fall off automatically.[3]

Once we recognize this basic function of our reality, we can direct our attention and energy towards the _growth-process_ instead of striving for a fleeting and illusionary stability of our material environment. With this understanding we will then interpret the purpose of any change within us or outside us as _an alignment towards something new_, even if these changes may initially cause disorientation and confusion.

Confidence in the purpose of reality is the fundamental conviction that _all_ events we confront in our present state of corporeal existence do have the purpose to awaken us to our immense abilities, so we

---

[3] This is the reason why the accumulation of material objects - as the modern media propagate - hardly ever produces the promised permanent satisfaction. After our initial joy of buying wears off, we often are disappointed how little happiness the purchase of a new thing brings us. All too soon a feeling of unfulfilled desire prompts us to again crave new objects and experiences.

People able to fulfill all their material desires, but lacking orientation beyond matter, often lose themselves in activities that do not advance their development (e.g. the unshackled accumulation of material objects or money, charitable activities without real inner engagement, participation in social circles directed towards superficialities etc.). The feeling of boredom and meaninglessness of material existence that often surrounds this type of people is an excellent proof that reality is directed towards inner growth and not towards the stability of our outer environment.

may explore them, understand them and use them for our further growth.

We experience this confidence when we e.g. feel the impulse for an endeavor, initiate the action that starts the project and then - once we have done everything within our power - leave it to the purpose of reality to 'produce' the experiences we intend to receive.

Already now this confidence works exceptionally well on several levels of our life. For any bodily movement - e.g. to pull a book from a shelf - we only think that we want to hold the book in our hand, but never what muscles to contract, how to keep our balance etc. - When we e.g. go to an important meeting, we only have our objective (our intentions) in mind, but hardly ever think about what words to use. This confidence that works perfectly on many levels can easily be extended to all other areas of life.

Even if some of our ideas and impulses do not manifest exactly as imagined, it is especially these 'failed' undertakings that inform us - often in a highly instructive way - where our ideas do not agree with reality. This 'negative' feed-back eventually produces a far clearer and more realistic perception how this world functions.

And even if much time passes between our initial activities and the moment we experience results, in the end it _always_ becomes clear that the apparent 'delay' was absolutely necessary. How often do we first need to reach a certain maturity before becoming able to gain impartial insight into _all_ consequences an endeavor of ours will produce.

Confidence in the purpose of reality is the fundamental conviction that the immense potential we feel within us will become real. It means to direct our attention towards the experience of more advanced states of consciousness - irrespective how fleeting they are initially - and then to actively bring about their unfoldment and stabilization. It means to consciously invest our energy into ventures that make us explore unknown areas of life. It means to trust fundamentally that these ventures will enrich us - no matter what the outcome - and that none of this energy will ever be lost.

This confidence is not brought about by blind faith or mere intellectual understanding, but only by us _experiencing_ it on a personal level. A skeptical attitude during our initial experimenting with this concept does not obstruct the process. We usually experience positive effects after only a short time, even if not every single effort in this direction does yield results. Growing freedom from events we thought inevitable before, independence from restrictive persons or circumstances and the additional energy and inspiration available for our life and development are first concrete results that encourage us to continue into this direction of total self-determination.

Any obstacles we confront on this path are caused by our very own emotions, prejudices and bias. What mechanisms give rise to these obstacles and how we can dissolve them is described in 'KARMA - THE MECHANISM' - the part of the Tattvarthasutra that deals with the practical application of this knowledge.

Confidence in the purpose of realty (_samyag darshana_) and intuitive orientation towards growth - the practical expression of this trust - unfolds in two stages.

- The first stage is still deeply marked by our physical environment that almost hypnotically confines our consciousness to the lower stages of development[4] (_gunasthanas_). Here we experience our orientation towards growth mainly as a narrow path that leads out of our hypnotic fascination with matter. It appears to us like a tunnel that - on our way to higher levels - leads through an increasingly absurd world[5]. Since this absurd world sometimes causes fear, we hold fast onto our path like to a lifeline. Our orientation towards growth serves to _counterbalance_ all the

---

[4] see '14 STAGES OF DEVELOPMENT'

[5] Our own world appears so unfamiliar to us, because we now perceive it from a new, distanced perspective.

unsettling events, environments and emotions we experience in these lower stages.

Yet the more our understanding of the confused happenings around us grows, the more we feel loving compassion for all those who still experience this mixed up world without real orientation. The impulse to lead these others out of their daze is another characteristic of this first stage.

- <u>Once we reach the second stage</u> of *samyag darshana*, we step out of the narrow tunnel the physical reality had spun around our consciousness. Our orientation shifts from leaving confining emotional and material circumstances to attaining and experiencing the fantastic reality we now feel expanding within us.

Before us stretches the real vastness of our consciousness. We begin to sense its infinite promise and explore this potential with an assuredness never before experienced. At this very moment we realize that <u>all</u> events we ever confronted led us to exactly this exulted point. From here onwards we pursue our path in unshakable certainty that *everything* ever happening to us will only support the further unfoldment of our abilities.

This second type of *samyag darshana* arises from the tenth stage of development onward. Its unfoldment now is inspired by the ever increasing clarity of our consciousness only.

SUTRA 3

तन्निसर्गादधिगमाद्वा ॥ ३ ॥

Tannisargadadhigamadva (3)

Confidence in the purpose of reality and orientation towards growth (*samyag darshana*) arise either

- intuitively (*nisarga*) or

- when we acquire a special kind of knowledge (*adhigama*). (3)

<u>**Intuition that activates our orientation towards growth**</u> (*nisarga*) is of an entirely different character than normal intuition.

<u>Normal intuition</u> is frequently accompanied by conflicting emotions: More often than not our premonitions conflict with our ideas how situations and events should happen. We usually are unwilling to reassess plans or opinions only because of some vague foreboding. Using the power of our intellect we try to overrule our heart and to rationalize this kind of ominous intuition as unfounded and illogical.

This conflict between intellect and emotion characterizes all normal intuition: we never know if we should follow it or not, too often have we been led astray. And - irrespective of how often our intuition had been right, - feelings of doubt and insecurity accompany this process and will continue to be there in the future.

<u>Intuition that causes us to orient towards growth (*samyag darshana*)</u> differs fundamentally from uncertain premonition.

When we intuitively orient towards growth, we neither feel doubt nor hesitancy. We experience this as a sudden understanding, a crystal-like recognition of the blockages that only seconds ago obscured our consciousness. It feels as if we step into the light, are finally able to see clearly. An immense freedom caused by the dissolution of the obstruction is flooding our heart, - an elation always accompanied by enlightening insights into levels of understanding that eluded us before.

Any problem that previously overwhelmed our emotions and our consciousness disappears. It became irrelevant the very moment we reached a higher level of comprehension. This new understanding separates us from our one-sided perspective that made the obstacle appear insurmountable before. Though none of the physical circumstances might have changed, our disposition is fundamentally altered. We are able to make out a path to a solution; an emotional load falls off our heart and we start feeling the elation mentioned above. The more the intensity of the solved problem, the longer this elation may last.

Yet not only blockages or problems may trigger this kind of elated intuition. We also experience this thrilling orientation towards growth when we completed a particular theme of life and our vision becomes free to discover new fields. We experience this as an exited sense for future expansion and as the sure certainty that the new level will open up further elating insights.

When we acquire knowledge that inspires us to orient towards growth (*adhigama*) we feel a similarly exhilarating effect. Attaining this type of insight is entirely different than the learning of formal contents we generally associate with the term 'acquisition of knowledge'.

When we read or hear descriptions how to expand our consciousness, we often break through to a dynamic understanding where our mind and feelings suddenly experience an intuitive re-arrangement of thoughts and emotions.

This may also happen while we are tutored by someone more advanced on this path. Sometimes their mere presence can cause this effect.

The crucial factor that brings about this experience is the intensity with which *we* search for this knowledge and how eager we are to understand it. The more ardently and consciously we strive for this

SUTRAS   THE KEY TO THE CENTER OF THE UNIVERSE   33

aim, the faster our insight into new levels of consciousness will open up.

Orientation towards growth arises either through intuition or through the acquisition of knowledge. _Both paths are equally valid;_ both equally open up access to this subtle ability and perception; both produce _the same dynamic stimulation of our development_[6].

This means that at all times people were able to find their path to liberation _intuitively, without ever getting access to scriptures dealing with this type of knowledge_. The Tattvarthasutra states explicitly that the unfoldment of consciousness is _independent of any formal knowledge_ - and this consequently also means all information contained in the Tattvarthasutra. The real key to more advanced stages of consciousness is _our very own intuitive comprehension_. Everyone heading in this direction is capable of unfolding this comprehension from within himself in a self-sufficient way and at any time he decides to do so.

* * *

Confidence in the purpose of reality is the key to liberation. - But what is reality?

Many of today's people would probably spontaneously reply: 'Reality? That's - working, eating, drinking, sleeping, recreation, family, friends, television and vacations. What's the point of your question?'

---

6 The one and only cause for intuitive orientation towards growth (_samyag darshana_) to rise is the removal of inner blocks that prevent us from perceiving this special ability of our consciousness. As soon as these obstacles are removed, we spontaneously activate this intuitive key to inner expansion. It is entirely irrelevant whether the removal of the obstacles came comes from within ourselves (by intuition) or is triggered by outside factors (instruction by others, the study of corresponding knowledge etc.).

Both factors are independent of each other, - both may appear simultaneously. Since both produce the same result, it is irrelevant which one appears first.

And they are perfectly right: What they describe is their reality. It is one of the many possible answers.

But what about the following situation?

Every second billions and billions of stimuli meet our senses - the color and structure of the walls, the hardness of the chair we are sitting on, the different scents we smell, the sounds we hear around us, the dry taste in our mouth, some vague uncomfortable sensation inside our body, worries and thoughts that zip through our mind and heart, some unrest, emotion so fleeting that we are unable to assign it to any concrete experience - all this and much more reaches our inner and outer sense-organs. And how do we react to this? We close out this whole universe and direct our entire attention towards the rows of black letters on the white paper in front of us - and actually not even towards the printed words, but to the meaning that kind of surfs on top of the black letters and just happens to stimulate our mind.

So now where is our reality of working, eating, drinking, sleeping etc.?

Out of the billions of impulses presented to us second after second, we select a minute amount of material that we allow to get through to us, to our awareness. We couldn't possibly attend to all the rest because it would overwhelm our consciousness and block us completely. We _have_ to select. And this selection-process is so subtle, so automatic that we hardly ever notice it. Only sometimes, when we abruptly come out of a state of deep concentration, we become aware how much of our surroundings we had closed out.

Now, we might think that this type of selection is something we handle quite well, for example when we decide to read a book, to drive a car or to attend a lecture, - all of them activities that surely require a certain attention, a certain presence of mind.

But let's see what our consciousness is really doing with us and how little we control this process.

How often while reading a book did we have to go over one particular paragraph again and again because our attention was drifting to some other subject? We _wanted_ to read, but our selection process directed our attention towards something entirely different. Certainly, - the words reached our eyes, but they didn't get through to our awareness. Something was closing the book to our attention, even though we didn't want to.

How often are we driving a car with our thoughts here, there, anywhere, but definitely not on the road? Did we ever ask ourselves who actually is steering the car?

How often did we attend lectures - let's just remember school, - and our awareness wandered far from what the speaker was presenting? - Who or what made us leave the speaker's words and let us drift into a different world? It certainly wasn't something we controlled.

And these are only rather trivial examples. How often did we reject our intuition though it was yelling at us and later proved, it was dead right? How often did we follow our intuition? But who or what made that pro or con decision in each single instance?

What makes us draw back from risk, - or go for it? What motivates us to do things we do not want to do? What makes us say a glass is half full as do the optimists, or half empty, as do the pessimists? Who or what made all these myriad decisions that brought us to our present state? - Was it really the 'I' we seem so familiar with?

But what about those two, three important decisions in our life where we knowingly chose one particular path over so many others, - did we really have as much control as we thought we did? Let's just look at the motive that was inside us at the time of decision, the real motive we wouldn't dare tell others, the real motive that was the true emotional cause for our determination to go for a career, an adventure, a partner, for security, responsibility, for challenge or for boredom.

Let's just once - briefly - forget all those nice official reasons that so perfectly rationalize our decisions and let's look a little deeper than might be comfortable.

Was it the desire to impress the father - to gain his attention, his love, his respect, his admiration? Or was it the mother, the elder brother, the friend, or the old enemy? Was it the fear of poverty, destruction, of loneliness, of losing something? Was it the hope to meet girls, boys, others, because we had only little opportunity for that before? Was it the enthusiasm to achieve a certain goal - and who or what had caused that enthusiasm? Or did we only want to show others how brave we could be? -

Were we really aware of all this when we made these important decisions? Were we really clear about everything that went on beneath the polished surface?

No, let's not fool ourselves, - it's not us who are in command of selecting, it's the selection process that controls us. We are ruled by some unknown mechanism that puts thoughts, meanings, emotions and impulses for actions into our consciousness. And we can only follow. We have no alternative, no concept how life could be without this automatic mechanism, can not observe this process from any outside point of view. - We have no idea what sometimes presents us with ever the same painful events that tear up our insides again and again.

None of the modern material concepts of this world offer information about this mechanism. But reality is far _more_ than mere erratic swirling matter as Western science assumes. Our reality - i.e. that what we individually experience within ourselves and outside of us - is subject to far more and different influences than all the laws of matter might ever describe.

So - if we want to free ourselves from uncomfortable circumstances, if we want to steer our life on our own, then it is worth the effort to find out what reality is, - to find out _what really determines our life_, - to find out what controls our selection process and how to take charge of our life again.

And if we feel uncomfortable within the limits of our reality and want to break out, then it is worthwhile to ask where to find new, undiscovered dimensions of consciousness, - and let their exploration become the most fascinating adventure of our life.

Because of all these practical reasons, and not for any theoretical or mere philosophic pondering, the next sutra describes reality.

S U T R A   4

जीवाऽजीवास्रवबन्धसंवरनिर्जरामोक्षास्तत्त्वम् ॥ ४ ॥

Jiva(a)jivasrava bandha sanvara nirjara mokshastattvam (4)

- The individual impulse of life - '*that what lives* in a living being' - (*jiva*)
- the elements that do *not* possess consciousness (*ajiva*)
- the mechanism that *attracts* karmic matter to our consciousness (*asrava*)
- the *binding* of karmic matter to our consciousness (*bandha*)
- the *termination* of the process that binds karmic matter to our life (*samvara*)
- the *separation* of karmic matter from our consciousness (*nirjara*) and
- *freedom* from all influences that limit our innate qualities and abilities (*moksa*)

are reality. (4)

At first sight some of the components listed may look quite unfamiliar. Yet this description covers not only our familiar Western concept of reality that assigns matter a central role, but also includes all mechanisms that make us really experience life.

How little our Western, matter-oriented concept can guide us, always becomes apparent when we crave concrete, practical orientation. Once life confronts us with crucial, immediate and individual problems, all scientific explanations how the material and mechanical universe works are of no help because they do not address any of our emotions, our motivations or anything that really moves us inside.

The components listed in the sutra encompass far more than just the physical building blocks of our existence. They also describe what governs our actions, what determines our feeling and direction of life, our thinking, our emotions, and how much energy we have at our disposal - irrespective if these factors affect us directly or indirectly. The description gives us a practical key how to steer our life far more efficiently then ever before and how to become aware of previously unknown activities of our consciousness.

The first two components of reality look familiar: Our universe contains bodies and things that can be perceived by our senses. These bodies and things are either endowed with consciousness or not. The Tattvarthasutra calls the essence of consciousness '*jiva*' and defines it as '_That what is alive in a living being_'. All other elements[7] that do not possess consciousness are called '*ajiva*' (literally _non-living_).

- **The individual impulse of life** (*jiva*) _is_ consciousness.

It is easy to describe consciousness, even if there seems to exist a bewildering number of concepts for it. Consciousness is the foundation that must exist _before_ the experience of things, relationships and emotions. All thoughts, all states like joy, pain etc. need a center, a subject, a carrier to whom they belong and who experiences them. In short: A feeling necessarily needs a _being_ that feels. In-

---

7 The term 'element' means that these constitute original forms of reality that cannot be split into even more basic parts.

sights and emotions cannot exist in nothingness, nor can intention or thinking arise from nothing.[8]

The individual impulse of life - *jiva* - our very consciousness - possesses a number of extraordinary abilities of which we presently know and use only a minor part.

Knowledge is one of the most significant of these features. It gives us the initial key to the unknown part of our consciousness. Therefore the first chapter of the Tattvarthasutra focuses primarily on this theme.

---

[8] The current idea that life was generated by the mixing of material substances in the surf of the oceans is barely one-hundred years old. Though entirely unproven, this grotesque hypothesis is surprisingly widely believed in.

It basically supposes that chaotically whirling matter would generate a living organism that in an inexplicable manner 'emanates' consciousness like the liver secretes bile. Consciousness is then thought to be a subtle, ether-like substance that radiates out from the brain and illuminates a particular scene.

What the hypothesis does not take into consideration is that this still needs a spectator, - someone who really observes the scene 'illuminated' by the imaginary ether-like substance. In a similar way light by itself does not produce sight without someone actually seeing it.

This pseudo-material idea fails to explain even simple phenomena like memory, intuition and emotions. It totally ignores intuitive insights into abilities and knowledge that could not possibly have been acquired or trained during the present life (examples are prodigies like Mozart, Blaise Pascal, Yehudi Menuhin etc., whose extraordinary abilities were not gained by training and also cannot be explained by mere talent). For all this there must exist a basis of individuality that continues during time and is independent of material factors.

It is certainly everybody's own choice if he wants to believe in a model of the world that presumes matter as the central governing factor of the universe. Yet this model basically concludes that the continuation of the species may be the only possible value of life - and in the long run even this would prove insignificant. Those who believe in this speculative idea block all search for and access to a purpose of life beyond this materialistic model.

In the Western hemisphere of the world we usually regard knowledge as the constantly growing mass of external information. The sheer volume of this data alone seems to make any comprehensive cognition impossible.

But this type of external data is not what the Tattvarthasutra conceives as knowledge.

The Tattvarthasutra regards _knowledge_ as the basic nature of our consciousness. Knowledge is such a fundamental and inseparable feature of individual consciousness that it encompasses the source and totality of _all_ knowledge within itself.

All external information recorded in books or other storage media has no impact on us as long as we do not actively integrate it into our consciousness. All formal learning remains without effect as long as we do not transform it into individual experience.

Only when we _apply_ knowledge to expand our range of experience, - only when we use it actively to understand more of our world and to reflect and change our own activities and attitudes, - then only knowledge becomes an integrated part of our life. We then stop viewing it as something new or special, but apply it without being particularly aware of it. Without this integration into our individual consciousness and experience, knowledge does not become alive, but remains a separate component in our life.

Knowledge - as the Tattvarthasutra describes it - is primarily the _ACTIVE experience of consciousness_. In this it is highly subjective and individual. The mass of data the West interprets as knowledge is at best raw material that first needs to be transformed into lively, active knowledge by individual experience before it can become relevant to us.

But the Tattvarthasutra goes far beyond this understanding. It states that every individual manifestation of consciousness (i.e. every living being) carries ALL knowledge that can possibly be known always within.

Wherever we are, the entirety of all knowledge is always with us. The fact that we do not perceive this at present, is caused only by our own prejudices, errors, misconceptions and erroneous beliefs what knowledge is all about and how it should be gained. This bias blocks our very access to knowledge. It limits the bandwidth of what we regard as acceptable. Once we remove these blocks, our awareness begins to reach into regions previously believed inaccessible.

There is no need to visit special locations to 'receive' knowledge or to wait till we are in possession of 'better' insight. If we want to gain more comprehensive understanding and ultimate freedom, we only need to secure access to this complete treasure-trove of knowledge readily available within us. The path to freedom is wide open for everyone at any place and time.

How revolutionary this concept is becomes apparent when we consider the absolute independence we gain. Since all knowledge already exists within us, we do not need anyone - no church, no guru, no organization of any kind - to 'give' or to withhold knowledge. We only need to find out how to perceive what readily exists within us.

We all have *intuitive* access to this path. It is open for everyone without the study of any kind of formal knowledge.

Yet there exist external sources which offer information how to become aware of the mechanisms that lead to the experience of superior levels of comprehension and existence: These are the reports of those who successfully completed the path to liberation.

These reports describe 14 stages (*gunasthanas*) human beings experience on their path to ultimate freedom. Each of these stages is characterized by the type of karma manifesting therein (the kind of emotions we feel, how intense they are and what types of action we are attracted to), the time we stay in a particular stage, the direction in which we pass through and how much our development is stimulated. Because of these differing features each stage has a unique feeling and significance.

Knowing the features and mechanisms of our current stage enables us to identify the main themes that challenge us on this level so we can deal with them far more efficiently. We thus prevent wasting time and energy on efforts that would only succeed in more advanced stages.[9]

It is not necessary to _believe_ that advanced levels of consciousness can be experienced. A neutral, inquisitive attitude and an eagerness for experimenting is entirely sufficient for our initial steps in this direction. Once we experience first results - greater clarity of perception, faster detection and dissolution of limiting concepts, bias, prejudices etc. - we obtain enough encouragement to advance further on this course.

Yet knowledge is _only one_ feature of our consciousness. Each one of us - i.e. each living being - carries a breathtaking potential for love, power, abilities and the experience of happiness within. Though in most of us this potential is still dormant, we sense it deep inside us. We are capable of fully unfolding it at any time we choose. Once we start out on this path, it is only a question of time until this potential becomes our real experience.

- **The elements that do _not_ possess consciousness** (_ajiva_) constitute the (material) environment of our consciousness (_jiva_). This is matter, space, time and the media that support movement and rest.

  - Matter (_pudgala_) - is well known to us. It is the substance of all kinds of bodies, constantly moving because of its inherent qualities of attraction and repulsion and composed of energetic particles of extremely small dimensions.

    Yet the Tattvarthasutra describes even more subtle forms of matter present-day science is unaware of.

---

[9] The chapter '14 STAGES OF DEVELOPMENT' introduces these stages in more detail.

- Space (*akasha*) - The Tattvarthasutra uses the unit *pradesha* ('spacepoint') to describe spatial dimensions. *pradesha* denotes the 'smallest possible extent of the element space'[10]. Yet other elements (e.g. matter) may assume far subtler forms than space and therefore are much smaller than one spacepoint.

  According to the Tattvarthasutra space can neither expand nor contract. Its primary purpose is to enable the existence and the expansion and contraction of the other elements.

- Time (*kala*) - is seen from two different perspectives:

  From the perspective of practical usage (*vyavahara-naya*) time is partitioned into present, past and future. Time is the medium that allows the other elements to exist in continuity and to undergo changes during the manifestation of their characteristics. Time supports the movement of the elements and in this context enables the experience of consecutive events.

  From the perspective of the all-comprehensive underlying reality (*nischaya-naya*) time exists as an eternal present. It does not extend into future or past, which are basically only limiting concepts we project onto time. From this perspective time exists in every spacepoint (*pradesha*), yet has no spatial dimension on its own and does not react or combine with other units of time or with any of the other elements.

- The medium that supports movement (*dharma*), may appear strange at first sight, but is easily illustrated by the following analogy: Water is the medium that supports the movement of fishes, but in itself is not their movement.

- The medium that supports rest (*adharma*) is equally illustrated by an analogy: It is pictured as the shadow of a tree that invites for a rest beneath it, but in itself is not this rest.

---

10 *pradesha* is defined as the space taken up by an indivisible elementary particle (*paramanu*). *paramanus* are far smaller than an atom.

Chapter 5 of the Tattvarthasutra extensively describes the non-living (*ajiva*) elements. Therefore they are not elaborated here.

Matter, space and time are the only three elements Western science is concerned about at present.[11] Science limits itself mainly to researching and describing our material environment. It directs the major part of its efforts to structure this environment in the best possible way according to its concepts. Yet the Western scientific model has no idea in which direction we may develop *after* we achieve optimal material comfort.

The elements *jiva* (consciousness) and *ajiva* (the non-living elements) constitute the universe. If they existed separate from each other, no further description would be necessary.

Yet within us and in our environment we constantly observe interactions between consciousness and the non-living elements. These interactions and the results they produce are an essential part of our reality. The elements *jiva* (consciousness) and *ajiva* (matter, space, time etc.) *alone* cannot adequately explain these interactions. Any complete description of reality therefore also needs to state:

- how consciousness (*jiva*) attracts elements without the impulse of life (matter, space, time etc. - *ajiva*) to itself

- how this attraction develops into the firm bond (attachment) between consciousness and matter, space, time etc. we continuously observe in the world

- what ends the growing of this bond, so that it does not increase infinitely,

---

[11] Though some branches of science are interested in mechanisms of learning, sense-perception and motivation, modern psychology is mainly content to collect statistical data about behavior and perception to predict future conduct (much of it for the purpose of commercial advertisement and the promotion of products). Yet this empirical endeavor does not pursue an independent approach that goes beyond the matter-oriented theory of evolution.

- what separates our consciousness from matter, space etc. and
- what we experience when we free our consciousness from all attachment to matter, space, time etc.

The basic factor that connects all these five mechanisms is _action_ - our very own day-to-day activities.

Yet by action the Tattvarthasutra does not only mean the movement of living beings or matter, but also some kind of _'interactive field'_ that all action creates inside and around living beings. This 'interactive field' is shaped by our intentions, motives, desires and the emotional content and 'drive' with which we conduct our individual actions.

The Tattvarthasutra unites all mechanisms that influence this interactive field under the heading _'karma'_.

Now, in the last twenty years the word 'Karma' acquired a somewhat dubious meaning in the Western hemisphere. It is usually attributed with a nebulous feeling of revenge of past actions, or guilt stored for future incarnations and often serves as a convenient justification of bad luck or inadequate planning.

Nevertheless - the fact that this word has been misunderstood and misused in the West has nothing to do with the validity, clarity and impact of the original concept of karma as the ancient Indian scripture of the Tattvarthasutra describes it.

This ancient Indian concept has _no intention whatsoever_ to chain us to events of former incarnations as the vague Western understanding falsely assumes. And - in refreshing contrast to many esoteric assumptions - the karmic mechanisms neither contain any mystery or secrets, nor need they be a negative load on our life.

The striving for fulfillment (manifestation, realization) of values and ideas originating deep within us, is one of the fundamental characteristics of our existence. We _want_ our actions to bear fruits, we want to _experience_ these fruits and we usually have quite real ideas, what these fruits should look like. When we e.g. strive to acquire a special, uncommon ability, we generally have a clear picture of the rewards we intend to reap - more social recognition, more control over our life, more income etc. The emotional power with which we pursue our ideas and desires acts like a magnet that attracts all components necessary for the fulfillment of these ideas.

Karma is the mechanism that enables this process to happen. Karma[12] is nothing other than the mechanism that makes us thoroughly experience the themes of our life until we gained optimal knowledge from them and our emotional attachment to these themes falls off.

What we experience is basically a neutral growth-process that we need not interpret in a negative way. The better we understand how this process works, the less we feel victimized by it. The more we can control it and the faster we achieve the results we desire, the less we will regard this mechanism as obstructive.

After describing consciousness (*jiva*) and the environment it is embedded in - i.e. the non-living elements (*ajiva*) - the sutra therefore continues to list all mechanisms that control our actions, - i.e. how our interactive karmic field works and how we can influence and dissolve it.

---

[12] The best key to understanding the original concept of karma provides the word itself. 'Karma' means *'action'* - and nothing other than *'action happening in the present'*.

The Tattvarthasutra states that our present individual karmic field always holds the *entire* actualized status of *all* our karma. It also asserts that we can change the character and inclination of all our karma at any given moment and entirely at our own discretion. *There just doesn't exist a shadowy 'mountain of karma'* in which supposedly all our past actions are stored.

True, the contents of our interactive karmic field were shaped by (previous) activities - as all our life is, - but this does not mean that it contains memories of all the *details* of all (previous) actions. The field only holds the *directions* in which we actively move (our desires and motives) and the *intensity* and the *emotional thrust* with which we endow our actions to reach objectives.

The primary purpose of this description is to make us aware of _all_ mechanisms that govern our actions so can employ them consciously and efficiently.

Yet over and above that the _sequence_ of the described mechanisms makes us recognize a far more fundamental dynamism that ultimately directs all our action towards a state where _all_ our karmic obstructions are _dispersed_.

- **The mechanism that attracts karmic matter to our consciousness** (_asrava_). These are the activities of our body, speech and mind. With our own actions, words and thoughts we attract non-living - karmic - matter (_ajiva_) to our consciousness (_jiva_).

This ability to attract karma is what enables us to experience the state of embodiment in the first place. The tendency of our consciousness to experience embodiment is one of the foundations of our life. As long as this tendency exists, we do have the right to influence this state in such a way that we can manifest the values, ideals, and concepts we feel deeply within us.

At the very heart of each of our ideals there always is a positive impulse. At our very core we never strive for destruction, but always for expansion, for ways to manifest the greatness we feel deep within us.

Yet all our ideals, values and intentions, - as high as they might be, - never justify _all_ the means used for their achievement. _Each single step_ towards an ideal needs to do full justice to its core. Each action that does _not_ correspond to our original aspirations makes us deviate from the fundamental direction in which we move.

All obstacles, opposition and problems we encounter during the realization of our ideas, serve only to correct our flawed concepts of reality and to break up situations in which we got trapped. It is our own will and our own consciousness that causes both these - positive as well as negative - experiences.

There is no reason to regard our body and its experiences as something base, bad or less evolved, as many religions do. And it is of no use to regard as valid only those activities that are directed towards spiritual goals.

A desire to turn towards new, more advanced levels of existence arises automatically when we completed the themes of the stage of development we presently reside in.[13] But as long as this has not happened yet, we should experience our bodily life without reserve. Any judgement that we might accumulate guilt and sin by this is entirely baseless.

Real growth is caused - irrespective of any concepts we might believe in - *always and exclusively by the removal of karmic blocks* - i.e. by the completion of the themes of life we felt attracted to - never by reaching a particular 'final' material status.

Yet real growth - the steady and stable expansion of our range of experience - can only take place, if we do not restrict our consciousness by binding _new_ karma. Freedom from karmic attachment is ensured if we orient our actions along the patterns described in the chapter 'FIVE FREEDOMS'.

Life _without_ action is no valid alternative for us, because we then could not release our existing karmic matter (our attachment to certain themes of life) through action. Life without action would cement our present karmic state and also our current stage of development (*gunasthana*) into eternal permanence.

- The binding of karmic matter to our consciousness (*bandha*)

Karma is not an inaccessible, mystic force whose inexplicable mercy we are subjected to. Karma is a kind of (subtle) matter that is present everywhere in the cosmos and differs fundamentally from the inherent nature of our consciousness (*jiva*). Though it

---

[13] Persistent feelings of boredom and general discontent are usually indications that our consciousness is already searching for new levels of experience.

does not possess consciousness, it has the characteristic to bind karmic mechanisms to our life.

Through ignorance, error, skepticism and strong negative emotions we attach this type of subtle matter to our consciousness in a similar way as the particles of our body do bind us to the material world which surrounds us in the waking state.

The activation (manifestation) of karma dissolves our bond with the activated karma. Dissolved karmic bonds do not effect us any more.

Activities caused by the manifestation of karma do not automatically bind further karma. Yet if we _react_ to a karmic manifestation with strong - positive or negative - emotions, we attract new karma, i.e. we attach new karmic matter to our karmic field that will influence us. This _renewed_ attraction can easily create a cycle of accumulating and discarding _the same type of karma_. In this case we usually get the impression that the same theme of life is occurring again and again. This cycle of attracting and discarding the same type of karma appears to us as if there exists a strong _bond_ between our consciousness and a particular theme of life.

It is important to understand that _we ourselves_ determine which themes of life we feel so strongly attracted to. It is nothing other than our own positive or negative emotional engagement that programs us to experience these themes again and again. Karmic matter is only the carrier-substance that allows this process to manifest in physical reality.

- **The termination of the process that binds karmic matter to our life** (_samvara_) stops the attachment of _new_ karmic matter to our consciousness.

The intake of _new_ karma into our interactive karmic field is the main cause for our confrontation with ever the same - limiting, uncomfortable - situations. As long as we are unaware of this mechanism, we unintentionally accumulate new karma even if it is against all our intentions and will.

The simplest method to stop this cycle is *to prevent the bonding of new karma* (*samvara*). This process takes two steps:

- <u>Step one</u> is our *decision* to stop all activities that cause the binding of new karma - it is our resolve to end prejudice, intolerance, laziness, skepticism, lack of knowledge, intense negative emotions etc.

- <u>Step two</u> is the *actual prevention* of the acquisition of new karmic matter. This happens automatically when we put the decision taken in step one *into action*.

Splitting this strategy into two steps may appear like superfluous exactitude. Yet we only need to realize how often in our life we make highly concrete decisions - and then fail miserably to carry through our resolve. When we - for once - discard the thousand excuses we normally justify these failures with, then we know with dead certainty that a huge gap exists *between our resolve and us actually doing* what we intended.

We only need to remember how often we decided to exercise our body regularly - starting 'tomorrow' - and then tomorrow never came. When we simply recall how often we were determined to slim down, to stop smoking, to drink less, to learn a new language, to tidy the attic etc. without us ever carrying through with it, then we know that it takes far more than just making a decision to achieve concrete results.

Only when we realize the immense power our own inertia and laziness hold over us can we assess realistically what enormous energy we need to raise to break this discrepancy between our decisions and action. Fortunately the same tendency that usually deepens our inertia can also work in our favor: If we get into the habit of *always* acting on our decisions, it begins to feel natural after a while to raise the additional energy needed for carrying out our resolves.

Apart from recognizing and eliminating the gap between our decision and action, we need to become aware of the mechanism that creates *new* karmic attachments:

If we want to prevent new bonds, we need to direct our attention to our very *initial attraction* to karma (*asrava*). This is a highly sensitive point: - All initial attraction to karma stimulates us with (new) activity. As long as we feel no emotional reaction to an event, no new karma is bound. At this particular point in time we often can decide freely how to respond to this stimulation. If at this very moment we recall our decision to stop the (beginning of a new) karmic process, and act accordingly, e.g. by consciously following a different (positive) line of thought or to refrain from re-enforcing a negative emotional reaction, we attract no new karmic matter. At exactly this time when everything is still open, we have the power to end unwanted karmic processes.[14]

Since we continuously manifest part of our existing karma - thereby dissolving its attachment to our consciousness - the total amount of karmic molecules in our interactive karmic field will inevitably become less as soon as we systematically stop binding new karma.

---

[14] A good example for this mechanism is the irritation we always feel in the presence of a particular person. Yet however strong our reaction may be, whenever we meet this person, there often is a brief initial period during which we are not yet irritated. If we take this brief neutral period as an opportunity *not* to re-enforce our sensitivity, but decide instead to maintain distance, equanimity and peace of mind, the chances are great that our irritation will either not rise during this meeting or at least be significantly less intense.

For future encounters we then have established a pattern of behavior that will eventually free us from our previous involuntary reaction.

Certainly, it takes energy to take this path, - more energy than just letting us fall into the familiar irritation, - but this is only a small price to pay for freeing our consciousness from an automatic reaction that in the long run will cost us far more energy.

- **The separation of karmic matter from our consciousness** (*nirjara*) happens automatically when karma becomes active (when it manifests).

The activation of karma converts its latent energy into a form that can be experienced. The activation dissolves the bond between our consciousness and the respective karmic molecules. After its activation karma ceases to influence our life.

This process happens all the time without us being much aware of it. Our attachment to the features of our physical environment for example runs on such a deep-rooted level that we generally regard it as a self-understood, absolute property of our life.[15] Only when we begin to dissolve this deep-rooted bond - from the sixth stage of development onwards - do we realize that our present environment is *not* a primary feature of the universe but one particular result of our emotional (karmic) attachment to a certain limited range of interactions between matter, time, space, movement and rest.

In the first five stages of development we usually notice the separation of karmic matter from our consciousness only when

---

[15] This means our emotional attachment to the perception of this world e.g. as three-dimensional, as subject to gravity (as our feet resting on the ground), as matter being relatively stable, as thoughts not manifesting without us putting effort into them, as nature being green in its phase of growth etc.

Though these perceptions appear so normal that we hardly ever think about them, they nevertheless are quite different to what we experience in our dreams. In our dreams we take it as nothing special when we fly though the air, when our thoughts manifest or change material objects instantly, when we perceive us as the center of multi-dimensional perceptions, when nature appears as a side-show that runs in the background only etc.

Though there is a present trend to regard dreams as rather irrelevant mirages, we nevertheless experience them as vividly as our current world once we immerse our consciousness in them. This demonstrates that our consciousness activates quite different modes for perceiving the world it focuses on.

they trigger strong desire or strong rejection within us. Though this is only a small part of all ongoing karmic processes, it nevertheless is the one part we can influence most easily. But the farther we progress in our development, the more we become able of accessing the subtler levels of karma that stand between us and the full unfoldment of our consciousness.

Our attachment to karma dissolves

1 - *in the natural course of events* as soon as the conditions for an activation occur, or at the end of the maximum period for which a particular type of karma can be bound to us. In this natural sequence of events a long time may pass between the original binding of karma and its final dissolution.

2 - *when we force its activation* - i.e., when we *intentionally* create the conditions that stimulate a karmic activation. This mechanism can reduce our amount of karma (i.e. the amount of our unresolved themes of life) considerably faster than waiting for its natural activation.

This is e.g. the intentional confrontation with someone whose power we fear, carrying out endeavors that demand courage and additional energy from us, bringing about situations in which we feel more alive, whose outcome is uncertain or that opens up a new range of experience etc.

- **Freedom from all influences that limit our innate qualities and abilities** (*moksa*) opens access to the entire breadth of our consciousness. Once we achieve this, we experience a state of realization that possesses such breathtaking depth and broadness - in love, knowledge, power, abilities and the experience of happiness - the Western culture has no concept to match.

We reach this goal through a self-determined, individual path on which we actively dissolve our entanglement in all elements that impede the unrestricted use of our consciousness. Once the last of these blocks is removed, we automatically experience the entire magnitude of our consciousness.

SUTRA 5

नामस्थापनाद्र व्यभावतस्तन्नयासः ॥ ५ ॥

Nama sthapana dravya bhavatastannyasah (5)

We experience reality (consciousness, matter, time etc.) on four different planes:

- on <u>the plane of names</u> - where we use names and terms for the purpose of communication and social mechanisms (*nama*)
- on <u>the plane of selection</u> - where we filter our individual reality from the constant barrage of billions of inner and outer stimuli (*sthapana*)
- on <u>the plane of all potentially possible features of the elements</u> - which constitutes the basis for the identical perception of reality by different people (*dravya*) and
- on <u>the plane of facts</u> - where individual features of the elements (or a combination of them) influence our actual present (*bhava*). (5)

We tend to regard reality as one holistic experience. Though we assign the themes of our life to well-defined brackets - work, home, leisure, study, vacation etc. - we nevertheless see them as different parts of one basic whole that always functions in the same way, irrespective of the particular activity we are currently engaged in.

Yet there exist <u>*four different planes*</u> on which we experience reality. And these planes function in distinctly different ways. As long as we are unaware of their mechanisms, experience shows that we tend to confuse them. So if we want to terminate unwanted themes, access more fascinating dimensions or change the general direction into which our life is moving, we need to become aware of the very factors that influence us. By knowing their particular characteristics, it becomes far easier to identify the type of action that will produce the changes we desire.

Once we stop confusing the different planes, we cease to apply mechanisms to planes where they do not work. Confusing the planes is one of the main causes of our misinterpreting this world's mechanisms. It effectively retains us on the lower stages of development.

We e.g. easily confuse the plane of names (*nama*) with the plane of facts (*bhava*). How often do we accept the words of others at face value and then become upset when their actions do not match their words. How often do we try to persuade someone with words who can only be convinced by our actions - which takes considerably greater effort. How do someone's words (e.g. a politician) excit us though he never means what he is saying and has no intention to act as announced.

In a similar way we often mistake the plane of selection (*sthapana*) for the plane of facts (*bhava*). We experience this as the desire to see events as we _want_ to see them, and not as they _really_ are. This prevents us from understanding that what we _want_ to perceive is only _one part_ of reality, not its entirety.

Consciously handling the four planes does not kill spontaneity. Though we separate the four planes' mechanics, our life stays one holistic experience. As we effortlessly are able to cook, listen to the radio and converse with others all at the same time, we can also easily handle the four planes while conducting all other activities.

- **The plane of names** (*nama*) is _focussed on the external part_ of our life. On this plane we assign names and meanings to objects, situations and events we confront. We do not _experience_ these objects, situations etc. on this plane. This happens on the plane of facts - *bhava* - where individual features of the elements (or a combination of them) manifest in the present.

  All communication with our fellow people happens on the plane of names. Here we deal only with names and terms. Here we exchange only names and terms.

  But names and terms are far more than mere naming, are far more than the mere words we assign to objects, situations etc.

Names and terms also comprise everything _we associate with them, everything that is triggered within us_ when we hear a certain word. Names and terms include all the concepts and meanings that come to our mind and even all the emotions rising within us when we hear them.

Only in the most basic interactions does the mere naming of an object express all we mean. 'Please pass the salt' is an example of plain naming. As soon as we attempt to express more complex contents and need to combine meanings, then the mere naming, the mere mentioning or listing of all the components we want to convey hardly ever produces the intended comprehension.[16]

Communication is basically an attempt to coordinate and align the ideas and concepts different people associate with more complex contents. But contrary to common opinion only a small part of this mechanism involves the use of spoken words.

---

[16] The question 'Who are you?' - as simple as it may sound, - is an example for the communication of complex contents. Is this just a request for your name or a thorough inquiry into your personal, professional, bodily and emotional situation? Does it express the hope for social contact? Is it an attempt to remind you of your innermost magnificent nature or only a casual greeting that can be answered by 'just passing through'?

Similarly complex might be the answer. Since all of us play many different roles in our life - the employee or boss, the lover, the husband or wife, the father or mother we are to our children, the expert we are in our special field, - we first have to identify the level on which to answer.

'Who are you?' said the Caterpillar.

Alice replied, rather shyly, 'I - I hardly know, Sir, just at present - at least I know who I _was_ when I got up this morning, but I think I must have been changed several times since then.'

'What do you mean by that?' said the Caterpillar, sternly. 'Explain yourself!'

'I can't explain _myself_, I'm afraid, Sir,' said Alice, 'because I'm not myself, you see.'

From ALICE'S ADVENTURES IN WONDERLAND

Most people are not aware that during communication they not only exchange physically expressed words, descriptions and explanations, but that they also transmit content on an emotional level. Whatever meaning we express in speech we also convey on the level of feeling. This level of feeling automatically reverberates with every word we use.

Our communication can be compared to an iceberg. The visible peak above the water corresponds to the words we exchange on the physical level. Yet the contents we really transmit equals the far greater part beneath the surface that is invisible to the eye.

The questions and answers we use in our communication inform us to what degree the emotional (invisible) meaning we transmitted _beyond_ words and sentences reached its destination intact. We employ our spoken words mainly to correct the differences that exist on the level of that deeper, emotional understanding. Yet we also encounter situations - often with intense frustration - where our words are totally inadequate to convey all the meaning we want to communicate, or far too crude to express more complex matters.

Terms and expressions used on the plane of names can be quite unrelated to their real meaning. Modern advertisement for example likes to use the expression 'You _save_ ... dollars' in an attempt to motivate us to buy a certain object. Yet when we accept this offer, we primarily experience a _loss_ of money and not an increase in our savings account as the word 'save' really denotes.

- **The plane of selection** (*sthapana*). Here we establish what part of our environment we want to be aware of. Here we choose from the constant barrage of billions of inner and outer stimuli those few impulses we permit to get through to our awareness. Here we build and maintain the ideas and concepts that stem the relentless deluge of impulses we continuously perceive. Here our selection-process takes place that filters our individual reality from a multitude of impressions.

This selective filter within us determines how much of reality we perceive and how clear or distorted it appears to us. It contains all the preconceptions and patterns we position like a screen between our consciousness and the outer and inner world. It further influences the way we see the objects and events we selected for perception.

On this plane we e.g. perceive someone judged ugly in a particular social environment as the most beautiful person in the world - if we are in love with him or her. Here we determine whether we see a glass as half full or half empty, i.e. whether we generally interpret events as conducive to our growth - optimistically, - or as a - pessimistic - confirmation of a general decline.

Our preconceptions and patterns may even be so far removed from the existing reality that we perceive the entire world in a distorted way. Drastic examples for this type of misconception are absolute dictators who feel secure in the loyalty of their people - until their fall makes them perceive a 'more genuine' reality.

On this plane (*sthapana*) we direct our consciousness towards those contents and values we feel - positively or negatively - attracted to. This alignment happens mostly without us being much aware of it. Yet we can fully influence and control this process. The Tattvarthasutra describes how to master the respective mechanisms.

- **The plane of all potentially possible features of the elements** (*dravya*) contains in inactive, latent form all the potentially possible features and variants the elements of our reality (consciousness, matter, space, karma etc.) can assume. It is a kind of blueprint of everything that may appear in our reality.

  This plane comprises <u>all</u> possible variations the elements can take on during their manifestations. We do not perceive this plane directly, since it exists as a solely potential, unmanifested state.

This may sound academic, but we often handle inactive, potential qualities in daily life. One example for this is an architect who presently is sailing. While on his boat his ability to build houses certainly does not cease. It continues to exist, but on a latent level that does not manifest at this particular time. Another example is a book decoratively positioned on a shelf, whose potential to convey ideas is inactive at that moment.

This plane constitutes the basis for an identical perception of reality by a wide variety of people. The functioning of this fundamental plane (*dravya*) is not influenced by the activities of the elements on any of the three other planes.

All embodied beings directly and intuitively connect to this plane. We automatically and subconsciously compare all our experiences with their potentially possible variations. We affirm intuitively whether an experience belongs to our particular reality. Everything that does _not_ agree with the possible variations is rejected and consequently does not reach our attention.

- **The plane of facts** (*bhava*) is _that_ part of reality where single features of the elements[17] effect _our present_.

Here we _experience_ how specific features of the elements really behave, how they feel like, what reaction they trigger within us, what meaning they convey and how to handle them.

Here is the anchor against which we check our concepts of reality. Here we test if an assigned meaning (*nama*) concurs with the real characteristics (*bhava*) of an object etc. Here we check whether the ideas and concepts along which we form our personal reality (*sthapana*) match up with what we really experience, or not.

And here finally the planes of names (*nama*), concepts (*sthapana*) and actual facts (*bhava*) can converge to form a _unified_ perception of reality that unlocks further dimensions of our consciousness.

---

17 and their combinations

SUTRA 6

प्रमाणनयैरधिगमः ॥ ६ ॥

Pramananayair adhigamah (6)

We obtain insight into[18] reality either

- **by *Total Perception* (*pramana*)[19] - where we comprehend the *totality* of the appearance of the elements (i.e. their forms, features and interactions) as they manifest in the present, or**

- **through *partial sight* (*naya*) - where we perceive manifestations of the elements from a *limited perspective*. (6)**

In the Western hemisphere we generally maintain the idea that knowledge is something separate from us, something that needs to be laboriously discovered by either experience, research, reflection or ingenious intuition.

In stark contrast to this the Tattvarthasutra regards knowledge as a fundamental and inseparable feature of individual consciousness. According to this understanding we always carry the totality of all knowledge within us, and it is only our limited capacity to perceive this that prevents us from becoming fully conscious of it.

Since the West adheres strongly to the concept that knowledge can only come from the outside and needs to be acquired, and since we almost never come across alternative models, the thought of carrying all possible knowledge in latent form within us, may appear utterly absurd. Yet the pride the West takes in the data accumulated during the last three centuries, overlooks entirely that we really have no idea how all these fragments could possibly fit into one coherent

---

[18] and knowledge of

[19] Since Western languages have no term for this type of comprehensive insight and perception, this book uses 'Total Perception' parallel to the Sanskrit term *pramana* mentioned in the sutra.

whole, nor where this rapidly growing pile of data might lead us in the first place.

In refreshing contrast to this Western concept the Tattvarthasutra introduces not only a candid outline of the structure, import, range and validity of knowledge, but also provides clear orientation where insight and cognition will lead us.

The difference between the two concepts originates in the fact that the West concentrates almost exclusively on only _one_ of the two types of perception available to us. Unfortunately this is the one type that only produces a _limited_ insight into reality (*naya* - see below). Over and above this the West further limits itself by focussing almost exclusively on only _one single aspect_ - the mechanisms of matter[20] - of the broad spectrum of reality and attempts to explain the functioning of our _entire_ reality with only the mechanics of this single element.

The Tattvarthasutra uses _both_ methods of perception to uncover an ever broader, ever more integrated, holistic picture of reality instead of splitting it further into isolated parts. The work reminds us

- that all knowledge recorded in books and other storage media has no meaning for us as long as we do not actively integrate it into our life
- that all insight can only be experienced _individually_ and
- that everything learned only formally remains ineffective as long as we do not transform it into individual experience.

The sutra introduces both methods of perception:

- **Total Perception** (*pramana*) - We experience Total Perception as the immediate and complete comprehension of complex situations as they occur in the present. As supernatural as this ability may appear to us, as naturally and effortlessly do we handle it in

---

[20] more precisely: the belief that reality is governed only by mechanisms of matter

our daily life. Without constantly applying Total Perception - *pramana* - we would hardly have chances to survive.

pramana is complete perception and understanding that with lightening speed evaluates multi-layered, interconnected and highly complicated situations for which an intellectual analysis of the many factors would be by far too slow. We handle this ability with dreamlike certainty, though we are almost never aware how complex this process really is.

One example: We want to cross a street. We see a car approaching whose course might collide with our intended path. In this brief moment - before we decide to either step onto the road or not - we comprehend the totality of the situation in all its complex diversity.

We register the speed of the car, the width of the street and also the driver's capacity to avoid us. We take in visibility (day, night, clear, cloudy or foggy vision), nature and condition of the road (dry, wet, icy, asphalt, pebbles, sand) and the velocity of the car in relation to all these components. We check if other pedestrians intend to cross the street before us, thereby possibly causing the car to slow down. The shape of the car tells us that this make is preferred by young aggressive drivers. Some - however vague - notion arises that the driver might be pressed for time.

We assess our strength and constitution to safely reach the other side - and also our readiness and capability to speed up should we have misjudged. We consider if we *have* to cross the street *before* the car, i.e. how far *we* are pressed by time, - a contemplation that connects us to even more complex psychological dimensions.

All this and much more we completely take in in the fraction of a second, weigh it against each other and make our decision with lightning speed and dreamlike surety. Certainly - the accident-statistics show that some get it wrong, but *we* succeeded in arriving here and now and this tells us how effectively we handle Total Perception.

We get undeniable proof of this special ability when we look at the many multi-layered situations we confront each day: - all the highly complex bodily decisions we subconsciously make almost every second; - the swiftness with which we evaluate power, disposition and strategy of opponents and then instantly fine-tune our tactics; - the immediacy with which we judge whether our outer and inner situation agrees with our deeper motives, ideas and values, and how we should react to this.

In all these decisions our intellect plays only an insignificant role. Certainly, we consciously adopt well thought out and laboriously trained concepts and action-sequences, but we also experience often that Total Perception - our direct access to comprehensive knowledge - easily overrides any mental calculation however logical it may appear to us. When speed of judgement and decision is vital to our survival, we almost always revert to Total Perception - to the one ability that brings us so efficiently through life.

Total Perception is the direct connection to our consciousness. Its ability to understand the most complex circumstances instantly and comprehensively, gives us a taste of the immense potential of insights that still rests undiscovered deep within us.

The casualness with which we handle Total Perception in daily life demonstrates how natural and spontaneous it will be to activate even more comprehensive levels of insight - we only need to direct this familiar ability towards _new and higher_ goals.

The ease with which Total Perception matured in our life - from toddler to adult - further demonstrates how playful the unfoldment of this ability can be.

And last not least: - Total Perception presents the irrefutable proof that _even now_ we do have the ability to reach and develop new dimensions of consciousness. We only need to extend the range in which we use this skill.

The range of Total Perception - i.e. how much of reality we perceive by it and how clear this insight is - mirrors our degree of awareness of this ability. Yet we do not need special training to acquire this skill, we only need to remove the blocks that obstruct its operation.[21]

These blocks are caused by our very own presumptions, errors and misunderstandings. They are the stronger, the more intensely we project prejudices, inaccuracies etc. onto the world and the more we reject, neglect or postpone to correct them. If we want to expand the scope of what we perceive through Total Perception, we need to understand that it is entirely at _our own discretion_ how fast and to what extent we remove these obstructions.

The karmic blocks that obstruct this ability also determine the clarity of our insights.

The range of Total Perception further depends on the channels we use to perceive our world. The bandwidth and features of these channels are described from Sutra 9 onwards.

Total Perception - _pramana_ - is our very key to more advanced, superior levels of consciousness. Only Total Perception is fast enough to evaluate the multitude of new impressions we receive during an expansion of consciousness. Only Total Perception gives us the dreamlike certainty to select and amplify only those impulses that drive us to further unfoldment.

It is primarily _the development of Total Perception_ - _pramana_ - that opens our access to new areas of our consciousness and _not_ the use of intellectual knowledge.

Intellectually analyzing new experiences is certainly of value. It can make us conscious of _what_ we encountered, connect it to previous experiences and generally give us the confirmation and security that makes us continue on our chosen path.

---

[21] KARMA - THE MECHANISM describes how to remove these blocks.

Yet intellectual analysis can only yield results *after* we experienced the new (expansion of consciousness). It is utterly impossible to *initiate* an expansion of consciousness by intellectual analysis alone, or by *thinking logically* about it. And further - any attempt to intellectually analyze an expansion of consciousness *while it is happening*, significantly disturbs this process.

There are two types of Total Perception - *pramana*:

1 - direct insight (*pratyaksha*) - is our highest form of Total Perception. We experience it *directly* in our consciousness *without the help of physical carriers* (i.e. without the help of external influences like sense-impressions, books or teachers).

This type of insight causes such clear and self-evident understanding of facts and circumstances, situations and interconnectedness that no proof by further factors is needed.

2 - indirect insight (*paroksha*) - we obtain by external means and carriers like sense-impressions, books or teachers.

Indirect insight may be flawed. Before we adopt it, we need to examine its validity.

- **Partial sight** (*naya*) - We use partial sight to explore and analyze single features of the world around us or within us. Partial sight is a precise instrument to delve deeply into one particular form or one particular appearance of an element.

Partial sights are limited aspects or parts of what we perceive through Total Perception. Partial sights always originate in *pramana*, i.e. they always arise from Total Perception.

The purpose of partial sight is to make us conscious of single features of what we perceived through Total Perception. Like with a magnifying glass we focus our attention to one single aspect of Total Perception - *pramana* - to investigate it from a limited perspective.

Partial sights prevent confusion, uncertainty and misunderstanding in the communication of insights. If handled correctly they also identify exactly the range for which a particular partial insight is applicable.

Partial sights (*nayas*) are valid for only <u>one</u> of the four planes of reality,[22] i.e. either

- <u>the plane of names</u> - where we use terms and expressions for the purpose of communication and social mechanisms (*nama*) - or

- <u>the plane of selection</u> - where we filter our individual reality from the constant barrage of billions of inner and outer stimuli (*sthapana*) - or

- <u>the plane of all potentially possible features of the elements</u> - the basis for the identical perception of reality by different people (*dravya*) - or

- <u>the plane of facts</u> - where individual features of the elements effect our present (*bhava*).

Partial sight further relates either to

- the *non-changing*, general characteristics of the elements (*dravyartika*) - like the feature of space to provide room for the other elements, - or to

- the *ever-changing* appearances of the elements (*paryayarthika*) - like the different physical forms we take on during our incarnations.

Sutra 33 describes seven easy steps to gain insight into reality through partial sight (*naya*).

* * *

In the Western hemisphere of the world we concentrate mainly on partial sight (*naya*). Our current concept of knowledge is essentially

---

[22] see sutra 5

an enormous attempt to split up reality into ever smaller parts. We experience this e.g. as our tendency to interpret observations and experiences as 'data' or as the effort to measure quality in terms of quantity.[23] According to the leaders of this trend of thought fragmentation is supposed to make the world easier to understand and to handle.

But unfortunately this shattering of reality produces the exact opposite effect. In the overabundance of details that flood us at present, we lack all orientation.

Now, - Total Perception - *pramana* - would certainly be fully capable of providing the desired sovereign orientation. Since we already are quite accustomed to use this ability for grasping the most complex of situations, it would be easy to also apply it for gaining understanding of the _structure_ of reality and knowledge as well. In this process we would easily recognize which part of the present pile of data is irrelevant and proceed onto more significant themes of life. A wide-spread application of this ability would be simple because everyone is well versed in using Total Perception as their main method to get through life.

Yet formal education and the modern media divert our attention from this exquisitely effective ability. Our capacity to instantly comprehend highly complex situations is regarded as so natural, so basic that we never even think of systematically exploring, training and - above all - _expanding_ this fabulous feature of our consciousness.

We nevertheless recognize intuitively that our focus on partial sights does not give us the immediate and comprehensive experience and satisfaction we are familiar with through Total Perception. Though schools and media tell us to only rely on partial sight, in real

---

[23] this means e.g. _digitizing_ as many events and circumstances as possible as our present computer-oriented society strives to do

life we use Total Perception - and this is the very origin of the great discrepancy between individual life and science. [24]

Once we begin to _consciously_ employ Total Perception, it unfolds new dimensions of experience within us that are far more intense, interesting and fulfilling than a life mainly directed towards the accumulation of objects and bodily comfort.

---

[24] The almost exclusive focus of the West on partial sights is caused by science. Science splits the limited part of reality it recognizes into smaller parts, and then examines them in the light of narrow conditions. Many scientists engaged in this type of research are idealistically motivated that this approach will produce verifiable and valuable information about features and behavior of the examined objects.

There is basically nothing wrong with this approach. No doubt, science helped to make the physical conditions of life more comfortable and this also explains the popularity of this particular trend of thought. But unfortunately this success caused science to demand that _all_ of reality should be explained by mechanisms that are valid only in the _partial field of matter_.

The propagation of this dogma is so successful that by now the majority of people accepts statements about the world only as true, when they are explained by the mechanics of matter. Though in daily life we constantly experience and use entirely different - non-material - mechanisms, this claim of science blocks the serious and systematic development of our far superior intuitive and innate capabilities already at the very start.

This overvaluation of the partial, analytical sight (_naya_) diverts our attention from our ability to effortlessly comprehend and handle the most complex of situations. It ignores the value and potential of _pramana_ and thereby impedes our growth.

SUTRA 7

निर्देशस्वामित्वसाधनाधिकरणस्थितिविधानतः ॥ ७ ॥

Nirdesha svamitva sadhan adhikarana sthiti vidhanatah (7)

We develop Total Perception - *pramana* - by

- **directing our attention towards this particular ability of our consciousness (*nirdesha*)**
- **by recognizing and accepting the insights we gain as our own (*svamitva*)**
- **by becoming aware of its mechanisms and features (*sadhana*)**
- **by discovering what causes it to arise (*adhikarana*)**
- **by consciously prolonging its duration (*sthiti*) and**
- **by allowing Total Perception to influence our life (*vidhana*). (7)**

The sutra describes how to expand an ability we commonly regard as nothing special into a tool to access more advanced states of consciousness.

The six steps listed are easily put into practice. They direct our attention to regions of our consciousness to which we have access, but which we never purposefully explored. They offer us a simple method how to systematically utilize highly complex knowledge.

The following description illustrates how the six steps can be applied to unfold our _intuitive orientation towards growth_:

- **Directing our attention** (*nirdesha*) - is the main key to _all_ new knowledge. As trivial as this may sound, as important it is for the exploration of _all_ new levels of experience. Without directing our attention towards new, previously unknown experiences, we will never go beyond the familiar limits of our life.

Our life is only where our attention is.

Our attention works like a spotlight that we train on events and objects. The objects in the center of the light we perceive the clearest. The more we leave the center, the weaker the light becomes and the more indistinct everything we see appears. The periphery of the circle of light finally harbors all the objects and events that we - consciously or subconsciously - deny permission to intrude into the center of our attention.

So if we want to discover new levels of consciousness, then the periphery of our consciousness - i.e. the *perimeter* of the cone of light - offers an almost inexhaustible reservoir of experiences we never cared to consciously examine. By placing them into the center of our attention (by consciously focussing the spotlight on them), we expand these experiences. They then become so vivid and clear that we can discriminate details and start to interact with them.

Everything we will ever cognize in the context of this universe *already exists at the periphery of our consciousness*. This also includes all higher stages of development. We have the ability to activate this treasure-trove of experience at any time we choose.

Directing our attention towards the events at the periphery is a conscious step. It is the deliberate decision to introduce new elements to our life.[25]

EXAMPLE: Many people experience orientation towards growth (*samyag darshana*) as fleeting moments of intense wakefulness, or as the sudden awakening from a daydreamlike state. Since they cannot explain what happened to them and because the events are so fleeting, the experience is usually ignored.

---

[25] Focussing on peripheral events might bring us in conflict with religious, philosophical or personal preconceptions, ideas or programs which often restrict our readiness for new experiences on deeper emotional levels. This does not need to occur; it is only mentioned here to alert us to potential conflicts.

Yet when we direct our attention towards these fleeting moments, they automatically become more intense. We now know what to expect and thus perceive them far clearer when they occur again. *Simply directing our attention* causes these moments to last longer so we can observe them more consciously.

- **Accepting the insights Total Perception offers us as our own** (*svamitva*) - means to recognize and admit that we really make use of a method that comprehends highly complex, multi-layered situations with lightening speed; - and that we can purposefully use the insights we gain to steer our life more consciously.

Once we fully accept that our consciousness is really capable of expanding - even if only for brief moments, - *conscious* expansion automatically becomes part of our growth-process. Accepting this by itself widens the scope of our experiences.

As long as we separate us from the events we perceive and regard ourselves as uninvolved, we have no systematic access to this instant and highly comprehensive way of gaining insight. We can only explore deeper dimensions of an event if we *stop distancing* us from what we observe.

Only then will we begin to recognize how deeply these brief insights into more advanced states of consciousness can stimulate our growth. Only then will we become able to detect and explore the new dimensions these experiences enliven within us to their fullest. We speed up this process when we familiarize us with the mechanics of this type of expansion.[26]

Though our present society displays a demonstrative openness towards all phenomena of consciousness, deep down below, it tends to regard any *real* expansion of consciousness as impossible. Despite the many books describing experiences of higher states of consciousness, we hold it quite out of question that *we ourselves* might experience something similarly fantastic. This needless atti-

---

[26] see sutra 20 for the mechanics of external knowledge

tude is caused by a temporary social trend that unspokenly demands that no one is to rise from the mass of people who might _not_ have these kind of experiences.

But this subtle programming and the resulting attitude that we are not _supposed_ to _really_ reach higher states of consciousness, does not take away our innate ability to experience them. It is only this erroneous bias that prevents us from fully exploring our very own experiences. It should be discarded once and for all. As soon as this programming is removed, the entire range of our peripheral experiences will be at our disposal without restriction.

EXAMPLE: We read the respective descriptions. We discover that the brief moments of clear awakening we experience are insights into the fourth stage of development (_gunasthana_), where our consciousness ceases to be mesmerized by the daydream-like cocoon that usually surrounds it. We come to know that one feature of this stage of development is that we perceive our path towards expansion (_samyag darshana_) in great clarity.

We accept that for these (brief) moments we really experience the fourth stage of development, - and that we really have clear, impartial understanding of our situation. We become interested in how to _consciously_ trigger this state so that our intuitive insight into the mechanics of inner growth will be less fleeting.

- **Becoming aware of the mechanisms and features of Total Perception** (_sadhana_). - The intensity and range of Total Perception expands in the same degree we become familiar with it.

To expand the range of what we recognize through Total Perception, we first need to get rid of distorting beliefs, concepts and expectations that have nothing to do with the experience itself. This means e.g. to discard the expectation that the rising of higher states of consciousness should always be accompanied by visions of supernatural light, massive expansions of space, ecstasy etc.[27] Expectations of this kind limit the range of what our consciousness accepts as valid events and allows to get through to our attention. While expecting a magnificent breakthrough - which hardly ever occurs in the lower stages of development - we completely neglect the many less spectacular, but nevertheless real insights daily life offers us continuously. Yet these everyday openings (sudden insights into our situation from a superior perspective, impulses to activities we've never done before etc.) are the very key to all _stable_ perception of higher dimensions of our consciousness - if we only pursue and amplify them.

We penetrate deeper into the functioning, features and purpose of our experiences when we gain a _feeling_, a _sense_ for their more subtle aspects.

Even if we are unaccustomed to directing our awareness towards our feelings and inner reactions, this new orientation alone

---

[27] Experiences of this kind are certainly possible but stabilize only from the sixth stage of development onwards. All feelings of ecstasy that occur in the first five stages are usually quite fleeting. They do not last longer because our attachment to the themes of life typical for these levels (karma) can only be inactive for a short time. Ecstasy is usually highly volatile and can easily be disturbed by activating karmas - i.e. by our attachment and desire for experiences on lower stages of development. Once we fundamentally dissolve this attachment (karma), our experiences automatically become more stable.

Yet as long as we are still subject to karmic limitations, the attractiveness of _any_ state of ecstasy is _based on the contrast_ between our normal state and the temporary insight into a 'higher' state of consciousness. Once this insight becomes more permanent, it matures into the _normal_ state and the feeling of ecstasy fades.

The state of bliss we experience _after_ reaching liberation is far more satisfying than any state of ecstasy that is still subjected to karmic constraints. There is nothing temporary in the state of supreme bliss. Its attraction is not caused by a contrast to lesser states, but by the perception of our innermost nature. - Why go for ecstasy, if we can have the real thing?

makes us aware of deeper dimensions of what we experience. This happens though we might not notice any immediate results.

To explore peripheral events for the expansion of our consciousness means to act on our insights, - to change the patterns of life we recognize as limiting, - to break away from people who steal our energy or direct our attention towards irrelevant issues, - to get rid of objects whose maintenance costs too much time etc. This new alignment concentrates our energy and focuses our awareness on the deeper dimensions the original expansive events offer.

EXAMPLE: When we intuitively orient towards growth, we feel a mental clarity that differs drastically from the almost hypnotic involvement of our consciousness in the chores of daily life. This breakthrough is always accompanied by a sensation as if we wake up from a long and intense daydream. The experience is very agreeable. While it lasts, we often remember clearly when it occurred before, and how much time has passed since.

As we probe deeper into this clarity, we become aware how few people around us look beyond the short-lived activities, goals or security they strive for. Our experience creates a stark contrast to their way of life. This contrast makes us more aware that the new dimension we perceive extends much farther than the usual objectives of daily life could ever reach. We now become curious how to trigger these moments of clear awakening intentionally.

- **Finding out what causes Total Perception to occur** (*adhikarana*) - means to discover how we can reproduce a particular state of consciousness (or event).

Two factors trigger the rising of higher states of consciousness within us. Both factors are independent of each other:

1 - Inner causes (*abhyantara*) - We experience more advanced states of consciousness as soon as all emotional attachments to lower levels, sublime fear of the experience of higher dimensions etc. that block our ability to perceive them, become inactive. This is the primary cause. Yet our emotional attachments

etc. need not to be totally dissolved. We also experience superior levels of consciousness when they become - partially or fully - inactive for a while. During this time of inactivity these barriers to our inner expansion are temporarily suspended.

We _stabilize_ these new insights by reinforcing them each time they occur, by _totally_ dissolving prejudices, emotional attachment etc. and by activating more of our dormant abilities. Sutra one describes the three factors that make this happen.

2 - External causes (*bahya*) - may also trigger higher functions of our consciousness. External causes can be events like shocks, accidents, deep disappointments, intense love, great pain etc. Events of this kind shake us up deeply and often stimulate a fundamental reevaluation of our current goals. They generally give us a radically new view of our purpose in life.

This can also be triggered when we meet people who are more advanced on their path to liberation, by the sudden recall of former lives, or when we explore knowledge that describes the path to higher states of consciousness.

EXAMPLE: We observe that orientation towards growth arises almost always in times of relative quietness when our attention is not immersed in the hustle-bustle of daily life and we have time and opportunity to reflect on us and life in general - e.g. during periods of waiting and silence, in open nature etc.

We discover that these moments of awakening occur more often when we intentionally prevent the intake of new karmas (i.e. when we stop refueling negative emotions, give up carelessness, laziness, indifference, put energy behind our intention to grow, actively maintain equanimity even though this takes effort etc.).

We now transfer our insight into action and e.g. read books that describe higher states of consciousness, search out the presence of those more advanced on the path etc.

- **Consciously prolonging the duration of Total Perception** (*sthiti*) -
Initially this is a basic <u>readiness</u> to explore ever deeper dimensions
of new insights as they arise. Yet as soon as our insights begin to
last longer, we should focus on preventing the intake of new
karmas. This is the fastest way to stabilize our insights into higher
states.

The duration of an insight gives us concrete information which
<u>stage or phase of development</u> we experience.

EXAMPLE: We observe that initially our state of awakening (our
intuitive insight into the mechanisms of growth) appears only in
very brief flashes. The descriptions inform us that this intuitive insight arises in the fourth stage of development (*gunasthana*) and
that it has three phases:

- <u>Phase one</u> is characterized by fleetingness. - We intuitively orient towards growth when all karma that previously prevented
  the shift of our awareness to level four becomes inactive (latent) for a short time. Though this awakening brings extraordinary clarity to our consciousness, our desire for experiences on
  level one is so intense that after a brief time (initially after only
  fractions of seconds, at most after 48 minutes) we fall down to
  level three, two or one.

  When we experience these insights repeatedly and direct our
  attention towards them, this process loses its fleeting character.
  In consequence the initial strong contrast to the familiar hypnotic envelope of level one diminishes. We now begin to notice
  that we lose ourselves less and less in the actions we are involved in. The clarity in our life increases and we become able
  to steer it far more consciously. Eventually we exceed the
  maximum time we can stay in this phase and thereby automatically advance to phase two.

- <u>In the second phase</u> some part of the karma that had only become inactive (latent) in the first phase, dissolves completely.
  We begin to see the limiting character of some of our attach-

ments, desires and preconceptions that hold us on level one. We stop refueling these bonds with new energy and attention and in consequence they cease to influence us a short while later. This automatically lengthens the periods during which we break free from the hypnotic envelope that overshadows our consciousness on level one.

- In the third phase we have no more karmic bonds that totally impede the clarity of our understanding. Once we reach this third and highest phase, we cease to fall down to any of the lower *gunasthanas*.

Since we intimately know, how long our moments of awakening last, we now can easily determine the phase of the fourth stage of development (*gunasthana*) we currently experience. We then also know what themes of our life (what karmic attachments) need to be resolved in that particular stage to enable further expansion.

- **Allowing Total Perception - *pramana* - to influence our life** (*vidhana*). - Integrating an experience into our life means far more than merely accepting it as we did in step two (*svamitva*).

As we reach this last step, we gained far more intimate insight into our new experience than in step two. We now know how much the experience enriches us and begin to use it actively in our life. It is a natural process that results automatically from the greater scope of insight Total Perception gives us access to.

EXAMPLE: We purposely apply our insight into the mechanisms of growth to explore unknown regions of our consciousness. We employ this ability in the same natural way as we e.g. travel to a country that is foreign to us or explore a new field of knowledge. This acceptance into our life now intensifies our intuition and opens up further dimensions of our consciousness.

SUTRA 8

सत्संख्याक्षेत्रस्पर्शनकालान्तरभावाल्पबहुत्वैश्च ॥ ८ ॥

Sat sankhya kshetrasparshanakalantarabhavalpabahutvaishcha (8)

Total Perception - *pramana* **- perceives**
- the existence (*sat*)
- the features and functions (*sankhya*)
- the place of manifestation (*kshetra*)
- the immediate sense-experience (*sparshana*)
- the time and duration of manifestation (*kala*)
- the inner purpose and meaning (*antara*)
- the presently active features (*bhava*)
- the extent, quantities and proportions (*alpa-bahutva*)

of all six elements[28] and their manifestations. (8)

Total Perception - *pramana* - gives us access to the following information about objects and events:

- <u>Existence</u> (*sat*) - Total Perception perceives whether living beings, objects, events, emotions etc. do exist or not.

- <u>Features and functions</u> (*sankhya*) - Total Perception perceives the components of the elements and how their manifestations are organized.

- <u>Place of manifestation</u> (*kshetra*) - Total Perception perceives the place where objects and events manifest. This also includes the perception of their size and range.

---

[28] consciousness, matter, space, time, movement and rest (see sutra 4)

- **Immediate sense-experience** (*sparshana*) - Total Perception perceives how our senses experience the elements and their manifestations.

- **Time and duration of manifestation** (*kala*) - Total Perception perceives the time of manifestation of objects and events and also the duration of their manifestation.

- **Inner purpose and meaning** (*antara*) - Total Perception perceives what influence objects and events have on our life and also what insights they intend to trigger within us.

- **Presently active features** (*bhava*) - Total Perception perceives how events and objects behave in the present and what reactions they trigger in our consciousness.

- **Extent, quantities and proportions** (*alpa-bahutva*) - Total Perception perceives up to what extent the elements manifest their features. It also perceives how their particular manifestations relate to each other.

* * *

What we perceive by Total Perception is called *knowledge*.

Total Perception operates through five different channels. These channels give us access to different regions of our consciousness. They also determine how clearly and to what depth we perceive knowledge.

The next sutras describe the nature and range of these channels.

SUTRA 9

मतिश्रुतावधिमनःपर्ययकेवलानि ज्ञानम् ॥ ९ ॥

Mati shrutavadhi manahparyaya kevalani jnanam (9)

We access knowledge (*jnana*) through five different channels:

- **our senses (*mati*)**
- **external sources (scriptures, teachers etc.) (*sruti*)**
- **extrasensory perception (clairvoyance, telepathy etc.) (*avadhi*)**
- **direct perception of the consciousness of others (*manah-paryaya*) and**
- **omniscience (*kevala jnana*). (9)**

Five channels give us access to knowledge. Each channel offers us knowledge of a different scope and character.

The channels - the five types of knowledge - are listed in ascending order, i.e. each successive channel perceives more subtle and more comprehensive knowledge than the one preceding it.

The advanced channels far exceed the range of the senses and the mind - the only channels Western understanding officially approves. Though we constantly use the advanced 'unofficial' channels in daily life, they carry the stigma of being suspicious.

Yet even if the West presently regards everything that works without the help of the senses as dubiously strange, this does not change the fact that the advanced channels are as available to us as the 'normal' ones.

Since their scope and precision reach far beyond anything our senses have access to, it doesn't make sense to refrain from using their immense potential only because some leaders of the contemporary fashionable ideology[29] regard the systematic application of these abilities as impossible - without ever having studied them.

We can use the more subtle channels in the same natural way we employ our senses.

- **Sensory knowledge** (*mati*) - arises when we perceive objects and events through our five senses and the mind.

  Sense-perception also includes the *processing* of this information by our mind, e.g. memorizing, recollection, deduction etc.

  The clarity with which our senses and our mind perceive objects is determined by the number of karmic blocks that obstruct the functioning of this channel.

  Sutra 13 to 19 explain the mechanics of sense-perception in more detail.

- **Knowledge from external sources** (*sruti*) - arises when we process and assimilate information obtained through verbal instruction or from scriptures and other media.

  Knowledge from external sources give us access to a far wider range of reality than mere sense-perception. External knowledge makes us aware of experiences our conscious understanding would otherwise have missed. It offers us concepts how to choose from the multitude of alternatives the one path that manifests the values and ideals we feel deeply within us.[30]

---

[29] the belief that the functioning of reality is only governed by the mechanisms of matter - science

[30] There is a huge difference between sense-perception and knowledge gained from external sources. One example: Consider the fleeting sensation of intense awareness when we leave the dense hypnotic envelope of level one. As long as we use only sense-perception, these moments remain fleeting since we do not know what to do with them. - External knowledge gives us an idea how to interpret and to stabilize this experience. We now can extend their duration and transform this vibrant wakefulness into a firm foundation of our life.

Knowledge gained from external sources always originates in sense-perception. Sutra 20 explains external knowledge and its relationship to sense-perception in more detail.

- **Extrasensory perception (clairvoyance and telepathy)** (*avadhi*) - provides insights into regions of our life inaccessible to sense-perception or through the external channel of knowledge.

Our present society regards clairvoyance and telepathy as such bizarre abilities that even the esoterically inclined think that this requires a rare and extravagant talent.

Yet as exotic and strange this channel may appear to us, as natural and spontaneous do we apply it in daily life.

Telepathy for example is nothing other than wordless communication. It is the ability to sense the intentions and emotions of others without first perceiving words, looks or gestures.

We employ telepathy when we e.g. enter a room where a group of people is meeting. Without a word being spoken, we perceive whether the atmosphere is positive or negative, whether the group is open to newcomers or regards our entering as an intrusion, and we often even feel what the subject of the meeting might be and the direction the debate is taking.

We experience telepathy when we steer a car and our passenger says 'go right', but *means* 'left', and we correctly turn left.

Telepathy is the wordless understanding between two persons who e.g. observe the self-portrayal of an acquaintance at a party and - without needing to exchange words or even looks - know exactly what the other is feeling at this moment.

Telepathy is the sure knowledge who is on the other side of the line when our phone rings. Though this may not happen all the time, it occurs often enough to be noticeable.

Telepathy is the sure knowledge of a mother, who knows unfailingly how her children feel when they are *not* in her presence.

We usually never call these experiences telepathy. And yet we transmit and receive most complex contents in a highly precise way without using material means of communication like speech, gestures, posture, facial expression, the arrangement of objects etc.

Certainly - these examples are simple, our ability is not always exact and stays more at the periphery of our awareness. But this is only because we never really cared to seriously train this channel.

Our present, rather naïve idea how telepathy functions, is the biggest obstacle for training this particular ability.

Telepathy is _not_ the transfer of single words or symbols, but an extremely fast communication of complex contents that happens on the level of _feeling_ and intuition. The main carrier of this communication are our _emotions, not our thoughts_.[31]

It is easy to train telepathy. Since we use this ability quite often in daily life, we only need to focus our attention on the extent and precision with which we already send and receive contents through this channel. Once we remove our erroneous concepts and prejudices towards this ability and playfully experiment with it, the bandwidth of this channel rapidly expands.

Clairvoyance also gives us insight into regions we cannot access through our senses or external knowledge. Through clairvoyance we perceive events and objects that exist outside our physical

---

[31] Our thoughts are far too slow for this task. We notice this when we consciously use words and sentences to paraphrase ideas that shoot through our mind.

In a similar way telepathy is not well suited for the transfer of single pictures, words or symbols that are disconnected from the dynamic events of life. And this is also the reason why most attempts to research telepathy with the usual scientific methods fail. As long as the current concepts of telepathy remain this far out of its actual range of functioning, no experiment will ever yield conclusive and productive results.

range at this particular time. Clairvoyance also perceives events that will happen in the future or happened in the past.

We experience clairvoyance when we e.g. meet someone for the first time, but get a strong positive feeling of familiarity - usually accompanied by the impression that we already have known him or her all our life. In this case we either have intuitive insight into the positive energy that any future association with this person will bring us, or we perceive strong positive emotions generated in other realities that are not bound to the time and space of our current embodiment.

This type of insight certainly also informs us about _negative_ associations, e.g. when - at the start of a new job - we are introduced to our colleagues and know instantly and intuitively which of them will cause us trouble in the future.

We experience clairvoyance when we sense with absolute certainty that a particular path of action will or will not yield the results we want.

Further examples of this ability are premonitions, experiences of 'Déjà vu', the certain, unquestionable knowledge that a particular event has happened though we did not receive news about it, or the sudden clear feeling that someone else will or will not meet success with a specific project.

Without training clairvoyance is far less precise than its potential permits. It is trained the same way as telepathy.

ESP, premonition, the sixth sense, 'Déjà vu' are different names for our ability to perceive knowledge beyond the reach of our senses (_avadhi_).

Everything we perceive through clairvoyance and telepathy may also contain error.[32]

---

[32] this also is true for all knowledge we gain through our senses and from external sources - see sutra 31

Clairvoyance and telepathy (*avadhi*) register only a limited part of reality. Sutra 21 and 22 explain the six types of extrasensory perception and the range of knowledge they access.

- **Knowledge we receive by direct perception of the consciousness of others** (*manah-paryaya*). - This is a state of consciousness where we perceive the mental activity of another person immediately and instantly in our own mind. This ability is far more precise and reaches into far subtler regions than telepathy and clairvoyance (*avadhi*) have access to.

Direct perception (*manah-paryaya*) operates in a dimension of our consciousness where our senses (*mati*) do not function.

Our mind (*manas*) plays only an indirect role in this perception-process. It serves as field of reference, as background that reflects the degree of realization of the other person.[33] The real perception happens directly. During this process all separation that normally exists between the consciousness of two persons falls away. Any communication by external means (words etc.) becomes superfluous in this situation.

Scope and depth of what we perceive is determined by the degree *we ourselves* have access to higher states of consciousness (even if we are not fully aware of this yet.).

Direct mental perception (*manah-paryaya*) is an excellent tool for the precise transmission of complex and multilayered contents. It is the immediate predecessor of omniscience and not subjected to error and misunderstanding.

Direct mental perception rises automatically when all karmas that blocked this type of insight are either dissolved or inactive (latent). It arises from the tenth stage of development onwards. Prior to this it can be experienced during the state of dream.

---

33 An analogy illustrates this: When we say 'Look at the moon in the sky!', the sky represents only the background.

- **Omniscience** (*kevala jnana*) is mentioned last, because this channel starts operating only after we experienced the other four.

In our present time omniscience appears to be far beyond our capacity. Though we assume that a select few exalted beings might experience this state, we take it for granted that they achieved this only though great inner and outer hardship. Yet in effect we reach omniscience without any external means only by dissolving our inner obstructions.[34]

Though omniscience appears to be far from our present reality, we often receive a taste of this ability. These are the moments between dream and waking when we have neither left one world completely yet nor are quite conscious of the other one. Here we often experience seconds or minutes where we command immensely complex knowledge that would solve all the riddles of the world if we could only take it with us.

Even if after waking up completely we shake our head with incredulity and discard the experience because we can't explain it, that whiff of multidimensional insight nevertheless was real while it lasted. We definitely felt it, however fleeting it may have been. It is no less authentic only because we did not experience it during the waking state.

We certainly can activate omniscience in our waking state as well. Yet we first have to significantly expand our current limited capacity for multidimensional insights before we could utilize it in any way.

This taste of omniscience tells us how natural, comfortably and without awe we handle this ability - even if only for a short time and not completely in the waking state. It also shows us that om-

---

34 We reach omniscience (*kevala jnana*) - and direct mental perception (*manah-paryaya*) - through knowledge of our higher self. Knowledge of our higher self means to sense the eternal, majestic being we really are beyond the limits of this universe (see '14 STAGES OF DEVELOPMENT' - stage 11).

niscience is much less alien to us and far more accessible that we ever thought possible.

S U T R A   1 0

तत्प्रमाणे ॥ १० ॥

Tatpramane (10)

All five channels of knowledge operate with Total Perception - *pramana*. (10)

All knowledge we perceive through our senses, from external sources, through clairvoyance and telepathy, direct mental perception and omniscience, is Total Perception - *pramana*.

This statement sounds almost redundantly simple, yet it has far reaching consequences.

It basically says that *knowledge is only WHAT WE PERCEIVE OF IT IN THE PRESENT*.

It says that knowledge is only *what we are able to access AT A PARTICULAR MOMENT IN TIME*.

It means that no matter how hard we try to memorize one particular information or train a certain reaction, if this information or reaction is not present at the very moment we need it, it is not knowledge. No matter how well we learnt or how often we practiced it, if it is blocked from our consciousness when we want to access it, it might as well not exist at all.[35]

---

35 We all experienced this e.g. at the time of exams, when to our horror knowledge we studied for months or even years suddenly is blanked from our consciousness. This indicates that our concept of knowledge and learning is flawed. It drastically demonstrates that merely cramming data into our memory does not produce knowledge.

It shows that all we want to really learn we need to integrate into our consciousness by *comprehending* it. It means that we first need to

Knowledge is _not_ the mass of information collected in books and other storage media we usually regard as knowledge. This mass of data is at best raw material that becomes knowledge only when we actively integrate it into our consciousness.[36]

Knowledge is an individual _experience_ we create for ourselves through the degree we open our own consciousness.

We obtain knowledge by _expanding our ability to understand_, not by accumulating formal data.[37] We expand our ability to understand by removing the obstacles (prejudices, flawed concepts etc.) that limit our consciousness.

The activation of knowledge - the moment of understanding - triggers deep satisfaction within us. Knowledge dissolves insecurity, error and hesitation and produces inner calmness, clarity, assuredness and security that is in stark contrast to any prior state of mind and

---

establish an overall framework of understanding so that all single pieces of data we later learn, will link into one meaningful concept. Only by focussing on _understanding_ and not on memorizing (learning) alone can we make sure that a particular knowledge will be available at all times.

[36] Knowledge not only consists of all the details a particular situation moves into the center of our awareness. It also encompasses the vast sum of past insights and experiences we _previously_ integrated into our consciousness. In any situation we experience, these insights support our cognition invisibly from the background.

When we steer our life, we constantly access this 'invisible', previously integrated knowledge. And even if we are not aware of many of the details, this does not diminish our skill to use them.

Riding a bicycle illustrates this process. This state of wobbly balance becomes possible because we continuously refer to all the skill we acquired on previous rides. Yet though this constant recollection runs subconsciously in the background, it does not take energy away from our foreground activities. It does e.g. not prevent us from focussing on finding the right way while steering the bike through unknown territory.

[37] Learning formal knowledge may have its purposes. But for the experience of higher states of consciousness - the theme of this book - it is hardly relevant.

heart. _The rising of higher states of consciousness is nothing other than the experience how knowledge activates within us._

The widespread opinion that knowledge can _only be gained through our senses_, is wrong. Too often do we receive - by way of sudden intuitive insight - knowledge of objects and events that are hidden or far away, but certainly not in contact with our senses. Too often we act spontaneously and intuitively in a way we never 'trained' before. Too often we access and use knowledge we didn't even know we had within us. And almost all reports of experiences of higher states of consciousness emphasize that these states arose without the help of the senses or material means.

S U T R A   1 1

आद्ये परोक्षम् ॥ ११ ॥

Adye paroksham (11)

The first two channels give us _indirect_ access to knowledge. (11)

We rarely become aware of indirect knowledge at the very point in time when the karmic bond dissolves that previously blocked its perception. Indirect knowledge always needs _an external factor OUTSIDE_ our conscious control to make us aware of the new range of insights now accessible to us. Therefore all sensory knowledge (_mati_) and all knowledge from external sources (_sruti_) - books, teachers etc. - is called 'indirect'.

The prime cause for the activation of indirect knowledge is _always and only the dissolution of karma_ that blocked our insight, never a particular event or the perception of an object.

The dissolution of karma opens our consciousness for a new range of experiences. Yet we usually do not become immediately aware of this opening. After the karmic blocks are removed we need _sense-_

impressions or external knowledge to trigger our awareness so that it awakes to the newly opened access.

Since our mind is capable of alerting us to a new range of awareness as well, we also recognize indirect knowledge through intellectual methods that systematically explore knowledge - deduction, comparison, induction etc.

All *sensory* knowledge (*mati*) is perceived by the combined functioning of our senses *and* our mind.

All *external* knowledge (from books, teachers etc.) (*sruti*) is perceived *only* through the mind.[38]

S U T R A   12

प्रत्यक्षमन्यत् ॥ १२ ॥

Pratyaksha manyat (12)

The remaining three channels provide *direct* access to knowledge. (12)

- Extrasensory perception (clairvoyance and telepathy) (*avadhi*)
- direct perception of the consciousness of others (*manah-paryaya*)
- omniscience (*kevala jnana*)

provide *direct* knowledge.

---

[38] According to the Tattvarthasutra the mind is a *sense-organ* made of subtle matter (*manovargana*) and located to the right and above our heart. *anindriya, manas* and *antahkarana* are synonyms for 'mind'.

The mind is an instrument of perception that - like our senses - exists *outside* our consciousness. It is *not* consciousness itself. Since the West is not aware of the mechanisms of direct knowledge, we regard our mind as the carrier or expression of consciousness. Yet this concept restricts our consciousness to the limited range accessible to the mind. This arbitrary restriction hinders us to search for insights beyond what the mind is able to perceive.

These three channels activate *automatically and immediately* as soon as the karma that blocked our access is partially or fully dissolved. We instantly become aware of the newly accessible range of knowledge. We do *not* depend on *external factors* to alert us to our ability to gain insight through these channels.

SUTRA 13

मतिः स्मृतिः संज्ञा चिन्ताभिनिबोध इत्यनर्थान्तरम् ॥ १३ ॥

Matih smrtih sanjna chinta abhinibodha ityanarthantaram (13)

- Recollection (of something known before, but presently not in contact with our senses) (*smrtih*)
- recognition (of an object known before, when the object itself or something similar or markedly dissimilar is presented to our senses) (*sanjna*)
- induction (reasoning on the basis of observation) (*chinta*)
- deduction (reasoning by inference) (*abhinibodha*)

are also considered sensory knowledge (*mati*). (13)

Recollection, recognition, induction and deduction are sense-perception (*mati*) because they are generated by the mind which the Tattvarthasutra considers a sense-organ as well.

Recollection, recognition etc. can make us aware of areas of knowledge that - after the dissolution of karma - became accessible to us, but which we never consciously explored.

SUTRA 14

तदिन्द्रियानिन्द्रियनिमित्तम् ॥ १४ ॥

Tadindriyanindriya nimittam (14)

**Sensory knowledge (*mati*) is triggered by our senses *and the mind*.
(14)**

Knowledge is the very nature of consciousness.

We therefore should be able to gain access to *every* kind of knowledge just by directing our attention to that part of our consciousness that contains all we want to know.

Yet our (emotional) attachment to limiting ideas, error, prejudices, laziness etc. - karma - partially blocks our ability to perceive and to understand. This is the very reason why we sometimes do not comprehend knowledge though it is directly before us.[39] While in this restricted state, we need instruments to access the insights we desire.

- The instruments for perceiving knowledge about our *material environment* are our sense-organs (*indriyas*). They make us aware of those parts of our consciousness that focus on matter. But this is only the outermost layer of our perception.

- For perceiving *meaning* behind the material data taken in by our senses, we need an organ (our mind - *anindriya*) that gives us access to *understanding BEYOND the range of our sense-organs*.

Our *senses* perceive their objects up to a limited degree of material subtlety. Their perception keeps constant for longer periods.

---

[39] At one time or the other we all experienced that we were searching for the solution to a problem and later realized that the answer was right before us all the time. We could not see it as long as we attached ourselves to flawed ideas how the solution should look like.

Our *mind* functions differently. It is neither restricted in subtlety, nor does it stay long on one single object (our attention constantly jumps from one object to another).

The combination of these two factors - our perception of material components and their evaluation - produces sensory knowledge (*mati*).

The mind is also called the *'inner sense-organ'*. Its evaluations of events, situations, recollection etc. functions independent of our senses.

S U T R A   1 5

अवग्रहेहावायधारणाः ॥ १५ ॥

Avagrahehavaya dharanah (15)

Sensory knowledge develops in four stages:

1 - **apprehension (*avagraha*)**

2 - **forming a first idea of what we perceived (*iha*)**

3 - **evaluation of our perception (*avaya*)**

4 - **consolidating and storing the perception and its evaluation in our memory (*dharana*). (15)**

1 - **Apprehension** (*avagraha*) is our first *conscious* recognition of an object after it contacted our sense-organs.

Yet apprehension is *not the very first contact* our senses experience. Apprehension is preceded by *darshana* - a highly delicate subconscious process that takes place *before* the actual perception-process even starts.

darshana is an experience that arises at that particular moment when our senses come in contact with an object for the first time, but do not react to this sensation yet.

At this point in time *darshana* decides whether a *'tendency towards the object'* will arise in the first place. Here the selection-process takes place that allows only a few of the billions of stimuli presented to our senses and mind to get through to our consciousness. Here - on this highly fundamental level - it is determined whether a stimulus will develop into perception and possibly become an insight later.

darshana is influenced by all the concepts and patterns we installed between reality and our consciousness. This filter permits contact with only *those* events and objects that resonate in our consciousness. Everything else might well exist and might even meet our senses, but because of this filter will never reach our perception and is thereby closed out to our consciousness.

Here is the plane of selection (*sthapana* - see sutra 5) where we direct our consciousness towards only those contents and values we feel - positively or negatively - attracted to.

Yet we are not at the mercy of this selection-process. We can easily reduce the effect this filter has on us. We only need to modify our ideas and concepts what perceptions are acceptable to our consciousness. We achieve this *by altering the content of our interactive karmic field*. This rearrangement happens in two steps:

- Step one is our *earnest decision* to give up ideas and activities - i.e. prejudice, ignorance, error, skepticism, strong negative feelings, laziness etc. - that erect boundaries around our consciousness

- Step two is the transfer of this decision into *action*.

We alter or reduce the contents of our interactive karmic field instantly and automatically once we put the decision taken in step one *into action*.

It is essential to transfer our decision into action because only this activates the particular karmas that prevent us from perceiving more of reality. We need to activate these karmas, because this is the only way to experience and recognize their character thoroughly enough to consciously dissolve them. It is <u>not</u> possible to dissolve karma 'theoretically' without activating it first.

We experience this activation as an intense confrontation with our own prejudices, pride, skepticism, passionate negative emotions, laziness etc. when we face new ideas, opinions and situations. Our decision not to prolong these habitual attitudes of rejection now stops this karmic mechanism instead of reinforcing it - as it automatically happened ever before. Only a short time later the last remnants of our earlier limiting attitudes are gone, the boundary around our consciousness dissolves and we open ourselves for deeper, more expansive understanding.

Yet reconfiguring basic patterns of our consciousness is not as easy as it sounds. Old, familiar concepts, attitudes, prejudices, inertia etc. usually hold such intense power over us that it takes significant energy and willpower to change or deactivate them.

As soon as *darshana* accepts an object or event as viable, it is immediately followed by a more or less clear perception (*avagraha*) that brings it to the attention of our consciousness.

EXAMPLE: Seeing a white object in the distance we know it is white, but cannot determine yet what it is.

2 - Forming a first idea (*iha*) - Our desire to identify an apprehended object stimulates us to form a first idea of what we perceive.

In this stage we select single elements of our perception and group them in a first attempt to form a coherent whole.

The result is an unconfirmed, yet distinct idea that an object must be either this or that.

Our perception reaches this point only if we <u>desire</u> to ascertain what an object or event really is, i.e. if we direct some more or less conscious attention towards it.

EXAMPLE: Is this white object a swan or a flag?

Many flashes of insight into advanced states of consciousness never reach this stage or take long time to be processed.[40]

Many other events also never reach this stage because we are conditioned to accept as perception merely those events and objects that proceed to <u>conscious processing</u> which happens only in stage 3 (evaluation) and 4 (consolidation and retention).

Unfortunately this (incomplete) concept of perception causes us to discard many ideas, inspirations and impulsive thoughts we regard as too weak to knight them with our attention. Yet we should never snub these subtle signals. It often pays to invest energy into vague ideas to raise them to a more conscious level of perception. Though the impulses might appear weak, they nevertheless provide access to more interesting and colorful experiences far beyond our present reality. - All great inventions and ideas started out as this kind of subtle impulse.

3 - **Evaluating the perception** (*avaya*) - In this stage we ascertain details of the object. We confirm what exactly we perceived.

EXAMPLE: We observe the flapping of the wings and now know this is a swan and not a flag.

4 - **Consolidating and storing the perception and its evaluation in our memory** (*dharana*) - Consolidating our perception means to connect it to previous experiences. We almost never store the <u>entire</u> object or event in our memory, but only those features that distinguish it from similar patterns already imprinted in our consciousness. While storing new patterns in our memory we always access past experiences.

Stored information supports a dimension of understanding that reaches far beyond the range of one single perception. By recalling previous perceptions from our memory we establish connec-

---

[40] It is possible to shorten this time significantly if we acquaint us with the mechanisms of consciousness and its expansion.

tions to other events or objects. The multitude of stored experiences creates a multi-layered and complex picture of the world as we perceive it.

EXAMPLE: This is the same swan I saw this morning.

SUTRA 16

बहुबहुविधाक्षिप्रानिःसृतानुक्तध्रुवाणां सेतराणाम् ॥ १६ ॥

Bahu bahuvidha kshipra nihsrtanukta dhruvanam setaranam (16)

Sense-perception recognizes twelve fundamental features of the perceived objects and events:

1 - **many** (*bahu*)

2 - **few (one unit)** (*eka*)

3 - **many kinds** (*bahuvidha*)

4 - **few kinds (one kind)** (*ekavidha*)

5 - **fast** (*ksipra*)

6 - **slow** (*aksipra*)

7 - **partial** (*anihsrita*)

8 - **complete** (*nihsrita*)

9 - **perceived indirectly** (*anukta*)

10 - **perceived directly** (*ukta*)

11 - **steady, permanent** (*dhruva*)

12 - **transient** (*adhruva*). (16)

The sutra mentions six features, but also includes their opposites. Our senses therefore perceive twelve fundamental features.

1 - **'Many'** or 'more' (*bahu*) - many in number of the same kind, or much of the same kind in quantity.

2 - **'Few'** or 'one piece' or 'one unit' (*eka*) - (the opposite of 'many'). This also means 'countable'.

3 - **'Many kinds'** (*bahuvidha*) - a large number of different kinds; e.g. the many types of goods offered in a market.

4 - **'Few kinds'** or 'one kind' (*ekavidha*) - e.g. a flock of sheep. This also means 'countable'.

5 - **'Fast'** (*ksipra*) - the perception of a fast sequence of events.

6 - **'Slow'** (*aksipra*) - the perception of a slow sequence of events.

7 - **'Partially'** (*anihsrita*) - we perceive only one part of an object or event, the rest remains hidden; e.g. the fate of a person who briefly enters our life and then leaves again.

8 - **'Completely'** (*nihsrita*) - we perceive an object in its entirety; e.g. a glass sitting on the table.

9 - **'Perceived indirectly'** (*anukta*) - we recognize a (new) object or event that has never been described to us before and is not marked in such a way that we could identify it directly. The characteristics of the object can be perceived only indirectly by inference.

     EXAMPLE: A man stands at a bus-stop. Though he does not signal, the bus-driver assumes that he intends to board the bus.

10 - **'Perceived directly'** (*ukta*) - We perceive a (new) object or event. Since the object has been described to us before or is clearly marked, we identify it immediately.

     EXAMPLE: We see a building that has been described in a guidebook we have read.

11 - **'Steady'** or 'permanent' (*dhruva*) - the steady and complete recognition of an object as it really is.

     EXAMPLE: All perception arising in a consciousness not subjected to error is complete and steady from the very beginning. It does not change at any later time.

12 - **'Transient'** (*adhruva*) - the cognition of an object is not complete and therefore subject to change, i.e. the form in which it appears does not last.

EXAMPLE: All perception arising in a consciousness still characterized by mixing error and true knowledge. It sometimes perceives more, sometimes less of reality and is called 'unsteady perception'.

S U T R A   1 7

अर्थस्य ॥ १७ ॥

Arthasya (17)

Sense-perception (*mati*) perceives not only the outer (visible) characteristics of an element, but its entire content, purpose and meaning. (17)

When our senses come in contact with an object, we not only perceive what is visible, audible, tangible etc. but experience an _instant and intimate connection to the entire basic element_ (*dravya*) of which the perceived object is just an aspect.

Elements (matter, space, time etc. - *dravya*) are inseparable from their features (color, form, size, function, duration etc. - *bhava*). Each time we perceive color, form etc., we always and automatically also become aware of the entire basic element(s) that triggered our experience.

This way we test whether what we perceive agrees with the possible variations that the perceived element(s) can assume. Everything that does _not_ agree with the acceptable variations is rejected by our consciousness. Rejected events do not reach our attention.[41]

---

[41] This describes how our sense-perception (*mati*) is shaped by the plane of all potentially possible features of the elements (*dravya*) - see sutra 5.

EXAMPLE: When we see a parked automobile, we also automatically recognize its ability to enable transportation - though the car does not move at present. This proves that the perception of *one single* feature (its form) makes us also aware of *all the other functions* of the car - i.e. its potential to reach other locations with it, to transport friends, to cause accidents, to pollute the environment, to give shelter from rain, and much more.

Yet the total number of functions a car can fulfill is limited. An automobile that would transform into an elephant does not fit the range of all acceptable variations. Even if we would witness such a transmutation, our consciousness would filter this event out and would refuse to accept it as a valid building block of our reality.[42]

That we presently do not *consciously* perceive *all* the features of the elements involved in an event or object, is due to karmas that block this part of our perception: - our own preconceptions, prejudices, ideas and emotions (karma) close off parts of reality from us.

Apart from the 'visible' and the 'potential' functions of an object or event we also perceive *why* these are brought to our attention. We consciously or subconsciously sense what purpose a situation or object has in our life and to what degree they are capable of achieving this task.

We perceive this, - irrespective if we accept this subtle perception or not, - irrespective if we like our perception, - and also irrespective if we react to this perception or not. Our consciousness impartially takes in the entire content, meaning and purpose of the manifested element(s). It is solely our own decision how much of this splendid abundance of information we use for our life and development.

---

[42] We would probably regard this as a singular event, as a distortion of our sense-perception or as a magic trick. But we certainly would not assume that all cars might change into elephants at any time.

SUTRA 18

व्यञ्जनस्यावग्रहः ॥ १८ ॥

Vyanjanasyavagrahah (18)

The first step of sense-perception - apprehension (*avagraha*) - perceives objects and events in an _indistinct_ way. (18)

Apprehension (*avagraha*) is our first step in the sequence of sense-perception (*mati*). Here we apprehend objects and events in such vague, uncertain way that we neither can form an idea of what we perceive (*iha*), nor evaluate or further process it.

This first step of sense-perception takes place irrespective if we later interpret, store or evaluate what we perceive or not. In fact we apprehend far more than we consciously process - much of what we perceive never passes the next threshold to our attention.

This process is another filter between reality and our consciousness. It works entirely different than *darshana*[43] (see sutra 15). *darshana* determines whether _a tendency towards an object_ will arise in the first place. In contrast to this *avagraha* (apprehension) certainly perceives objects, but only hands them to our conscious processing when the perception is _lasting_ or is _repeated several times_.

An example illustrates this process: A pot of clay does not get wet by a few drops of water. Only when we moisten it repeatedly, its wetness becomes apparent. In a similar way we apprehend matter that manifests in form of sound, smell, touch etc. During the first few moments we are unable to clearly determine what we have heard, felt or smelled. Yet when we perceive the event or object repeatedly, we become able to identify it.

---

[43] *darshana* is an experience that happens _before_ our perception-process even starts. It mirrors all the concepts and patterns we maintain on the plane of our mental structure (*sthapana* - sutra 5).

Conscious apprehension (*avagraha*) therefore happens in two stages:

1 - First we perceive something indistinct. Our attention is alerted peripherally, but does not focus on the experience.

2 - The perception happens again. Our attention engages, the experience gets clearer and becomes ready for further (conscious) processing.

As academic as this might sound, as tangible and harsh do we experience it during daily life. The current marketing and advertisement techniques for example prefer to transmit certain impulses only subconsciously, - i.e. they like to keep these impulses on the level of indistinct perception (stage one).

Though we might hardly be aware of it, even the indistinct and vague perception of stage one communicates *the entire* spectrum an object or event carries within (see previous sutra). So, if a vague feeling is transmitted to us on stage one that a certain (useless) object appears attractive, then from now on we carry a subconscious tendency for an impulse-buy within us.

The advertising company makes enormous efforts to prevent this vague impulse from ever progressing to stage two. Because once we perceive the content of the advertisement on a *conscious* level, chances are great that we recognize the uselessness of the promoted object. The spontaneity of buying the advertiser intended is then rendered ineffective, since we made a conscious decision against it.

Advertisement that uses this subtle mechanism is specially effective if it engages taste, touch and hearing, since indistinct apprehension (*avagraha*) is not available to all senses. This is also the reason why visual stimuli combined with sound (e.g. TV) are far more effective than advertisement using only sight (e.g. posters, billboards).

SUTRA 19

न चक्षुरनिनिद्रयाभ्याम् ॥ १९ ॥

Na chakshur anindriyabhyam (19)

Indistinct apprehension does not arise through the eyes or the mind. (19)

Our eyes and the mind do not experience indistinct apprehension because these two sense-organs do not come in direct contact with the objects they perceive.

The eyes e.g. can only perceive color that does _not_ come in immediate contact with them. Similarly there certainly is no direct contact between the mind and the objects it perceives. The eyes and the mind therefore have no indistinct apprehension. The impulses they perceive immediately advance to further processing.

SUTRA 20

श्रुतं मतिपूर्वं द्वयनेकद्वादशभेदम् ॥ २० ॥

Shrutam matipurvam dvyaneka dvadasha bhedam (20)

Knowledge we obtain from external sources (*sruti*) first needs to be perceived by our senses.

There are two types of scriptures.[44] The first type has twelve, the second one many divisions. (20)

---

[44] This refers to ancient scriptures describing the unfoldment of consciousness. These works are taken to be the main source of external knowledge.

Knowledge from external sources (*sruti*) offers far broader and deeper insights than sense-perception (*mati*).

It alerts us to experiences we otherwise would not notice.

It connects new experiences to our existing concepts.

In the multitude of potential avenues life offers, it tells us how to recognize the optimal path to manifest the values and ideals we carry deep within.

Knowledge from external sources is obtained through verbal instruction and by studying books (or other media).[45] Since we receive this information through material means - books or teachers - it is always preceded by sense-perception (reading, hearing).

Yet insight from external sources (*sruti*) does _not automatically_ arise when our senses perceive written or spoken words. We obtain access to this type of insight only by making a _conscious effort_ to _understand_ what we have read or heard. Thus it is only our longing, our 'drive' to open unknown regions of our consciousness that makes us step beyond our present limits of comprehension.

The energy we invest in transforming this desire into action and the strength of our craving for knowledge determine how fast and to what extent our 'inner scope' expands.

We accelerate this process significantly if we open ourselves to new ideas and concepts. But though this sounds easy, it is much harder than we think.

Opening ourselves to new concepts does _not_ mean to kindly listen to new ideas, consider them sympathetically and then - like a benevolent judge - decide whether we accept them or not. This is merely the (intellectual) evaluation of sense-perception (*avaya* - sutra 15). Any insight we might gain this way remains _on the level of sen-_

---

[45] In ancient times the scriptures were handed down orally. Therefore this type of knowledge originally was gained by 'hearing' and not by 'reading' the scriptures. The word '*sruta*' that denotes this channel of knowledge is derived from the Sanskrit root '*shri*' (to hear).

sory knowledge but _does NOT advance onto the far more intense strata of our consciousness this second channel of knowledge has the power to open._

To open ourselves to new ideas and concepts means

- to overcome our very own psychic barriers with which we oppose new and uncomfortable ideas
- to become aware of the emotions that make us cling to old concepts
- to make the effort to review and discard worn-out and limiting beliefs

even if all this makes us feel uncomfortable, takes energy and might require a complete re-thinking of the world.[46]

The starting points are easy to find. Whenever the presentation of a (new) concept provokes strong feelings within us (e.g. repulsion, stubbornness and even anger, but also fervent defense of our old models), then it is worth the effort to examine these (new) concepts more closely. It is exactly these powerful emotions that chain us -

---

[46] Though we consider ourselves flexible and receptive for everything new, we nevertheless hold resolutely fast to many familiar, but worn-out ideas about the world. Even if we - consciously or subconsciously - recognize that these worn-out concepts do not agree with many of our real experiences any more, we intuitively sense how much of an effort it would take to fundamentally reexamine all our existing ideas. Afraid to jeopardize our present hard-won stability, we dread the (temporary) inner insecurity that might accompany this process.

Holding fast onto old concepts solidifies our life into unmoving static that is easily mistaken for stability. But this static _will always break up_ - at the latest when our consciousness leaves our present body. In the state we enter thereafter, we clearly recognize to what extent our concepts agree with reality. We then judge for ourselves if we need further bodily experiences to access broader levels of understanding.

In future embodiments we thus might place ourselves in a similar environment as our present one to _again_ stimulate the dissolution of rigid and flawed concepts. If we want to avoid these recurring confrontations, it is recommended to react flexibly and positively at the presentation of new ideas _already in this very life_.

positively as well as negatively - to old concepts and thereby prevent our orientation towards something new.

We never proceed to new levels of insight if we expect or demand that these new levels conform to old concepts we are familiar with. Even if we feel uncomfortable or even embarrassed while confronting these emotionally charged concepts, this unfailingly leads to the discovery of new and superior levels. Exploring these new levels then makes the same fascination bubble up within us that in our early days inspired the discovery of our world with such enthusiasm.

When presented with new ideas, it pays _not to remain on the level of sense-perception_, but to make the effort to consciously advance these impulses to the far more intense comprehension the channel of external knowledge (_sruti_) offers.

This _conscious effort to comprehend_ dissolves karmic blocks which we experience in form of prejudices and limiting ideas. A neutral or positive attitude towards anything new therefore is an essential prerequisite if we want to move on to more intense insights. Any formal learning or mere intellectual understanding of external knowledge does not produce this access - even if it is taken from scriptures that describe the expansion of consciousness.

It is irrelevant which sense we use to perceive external knowledge. As the means of transportation does not transfer its characteristics to the transported goods, so also external knowledge does not become influenced by the particular sense through which it reaches our consciousness.

Knowledge that makes us recognize and comprehend _the unfoldment of our consciousness_ (_samyag jnana_), is a special variation of this type of knowledge. It arises if we allow our insights to be intuitively guided towards growth.

We experience this as a sudden upsurge of intense joy, - accompanied by dynamic insights that cause an intuitive re-arrangement of thoughts and emotions on levels previously unknown. We realize how these expansive insights intensify our growth and this infuses us with inspiration and invigorating energy.

As long as we are guided by our orientation towards growth, we exclude error, misunderstanding and doubt from our insights. While in this state, karmic blocks are unable to obstruct our comprehension. With unfailing certainty we now pursue only those impulses that give us access to ever more advanced levels.

Orientation towards growth is primarily caused by the removal of karma (prejudices, laziness etc.). Yet it can be triggered by the concentrated study of scriptures describing the expansion of consciousness.

Intuitive orientation towards growth might also be activated by the guidance of those who are further advanced on this path. At times their mere presence will produce this effect.

The scriptures mentioned in the sutra are ancient works that deal with the expansion of consciousness.

The scriptures originally were taught by the *tirthankaras*. *tirthankaras* (path-builders) are human beings who reached the state of omniscience (13th stage of development) and pass on their knowledge to others. *tirthankaras* are not yet free from all karma, but their liberation is assured.

Only few people become *tirthankara* because an extraordinary stability of body and mind is necessary to retain the bodily form after reaching omniscience.[47]

---

[47] The twenty-fourth and last *tirthankara* - Mahavira - was born 599 BC in Vaishali (India). At the age of 30 he began to strive for freedom from karmic restrictions and reached omniscience after twelve-and-a-half years. He communicated his knowledge and experience for 30 years before he left his body at the age of 72.

Mahavira's teaching vitalized the path to freedom and had profound influence up to the very present. During his presence as *tirthankara* he taught approximately half a million people and it is said that many of them reached ultimate freedom even during his lifetime.

The chief disciples of the *tirthankaras* recorded their teachings in extensive works. Successive teachers wrote shorter works that communicated the knowledge in simpler language.

The sutra does not list particular scriptures, but only mentions the number of categories these works are divided into. The categories are listed in more detail in the chapter 'ANCIENT SCRIPTURES'.

Here ends the part dealing with indirect knowledge.

The next part describes direct knowledge.

* * *

Direct knowledge is perceived straight, without assistance of external factors or the circuitous route of our senses. We receive direct knowledge through

1 - extrasensory perception - clairvoyance and telepathy (*avadhi*)

2 - direct perception of the consciousness of others (*manah-paryaya*) or

3 - omniscience (*kevali jnana*).

The first two direct channels give access to only limited knowledge, while omniscience is unlimited and encompasses the entire reality. Sutra 21 to 29 describe their mechanics.

Extrasensory perception (*avadhi*) arises from two different causes: we either gain them by birth or by removing karmic blocks that obstruct their functioning.

SUTRA 21

भवप्रत्ययोऽवधिर्देवनारकाणाम् ॥ २१ ॥

Bhava pratyayo avadhir deva narakanam (21)

In the inhabitants of celestial and nether regions[48] extrasensory perception (*avadhi*) is inborn. (21)

<u>The inhabitants of regions with celestial character</u> (*devas*) are beings, who by their own activities and desires attracted a type of positive karma that caused their embodiment in these regions. The bodies and life-circumstances of *devas* support their deep desire for happiness, unrestricted movement, health, supernatural abilities, stress-free communication, freedom from sorrow, fear etc. Since the 'celestial' regions are inhabited by beings of similar disposition, these desires can be satisfied without being disturbed by beings with different objectives in life.[49]

---

[48] The Tattvarthasutra distinguishes four classes of beings:

    1 - *devas* - beings residing in regions of celestial character
    2 - *narakas* - beings residing in regions of hellish character
    3 - human beings
    4 - animals and plants.

For someone born and raised in the Western cultural environment this division - and specially the first two classes - may promptly be relegated to the area of religious fable or to a rather simpleminded higher instance of merit and punishment.

Yet this type of mystical context is not meant here. The statement refers to the comprehensive classification of life-forms that is described in great detail in chapter 3, 4 and 5 of the Tattvarthasutra.

Western science - which presently influences most of our ideas of life - is not interested in these areas, does not examine them and therefore cannot seriously state anything about them.

[49] In spite of all their - from the human point of view - extraordinary abilities, *devas* are not free from karma. Negative karma that might oppose the life-circumstances of *devas* has only receded into its latent

Incarnations in regions with nether, 'hellish' character are caused by excessive attachment to objects, persons, status etc., unrestrained longing for the property of others, feelings like 'All this is mine' and revengeful, cruel thoughts at our time of death.[50] This manifests the deep desire of the being for further attachment to matter and for the experience of cruel, revengeful behavior. Since the nether, 'infernal'

---

state and will become active after the desires (the karmas) that caused the celestial birth(s) have been fulfilled.

Celestial beings can become so immersed in the enjoyment of their 'heavenly' conditions that they forget to develop higher stages of awareness. But here also the karmic mechanisms ensure that their (temporary) stability is broken up for further progress.

[50] Most people hold fast onto the belief that their time of death is far away. We abhor to think that we will experience death with inevitable certainty.

We further tend to regard thoughts and emotions as of little consequence since we experience such an abundance of them.

Anything we may feel or think in that 'far away' and supposedly 'brief' moment when we ultimately leave our body, we therefore regard of minor importance for our current life.

Yet the fact that _we_ evaluate this 'moment' as unimportant does not in the least diminish its profound impact on our future conditions of life. The point of our death is an extremely intense experience. Here all unfulfilled desires and all our ideas of what we still would like to experience condense into _one_ intense feeling, into _one intense longing_. And this deep longing draws us into exactly that (new) environment that enables us to experience the physical manifestation of these desires in the best possible way.

At the point of our bodily death all we only pretended to be, all we only made up before ourselves and others, falls off like a discarded shell. What remains is raw and real yearning deep within us that dynamically attracts exactly those components we still want to experience. This tendency to new or 'renewed' experiences we only shape ourselves through the way we conduct _all_ our _current_ life.

It certainly is everyone's own decision to regard his or her moment of death as irrelevant or to envisage it so far in the future as if it would never occur. Yet death is inevitable. And once we experience this event in all its intensity, there is no opportunity left to alter the tendencies that then propel us into our new environment.

regions are inhabited by beings with similar attitudes (*narakas*), this desire can be satisfied without disturbing others who have different objectives in life. Once this attitude weakens, i.e. once the corresponding karma is dissolved, someone bound to this level will get the opportunity to leave the respective region.

It is important to understand that these two types of existence denote no (religious) concept of heaven and hell in the sense of 'punishment' and 'eternal damnation', or 'reward' and 'eternal bliss', but a mechanism that positions us in exactly those conditions of life that are ideally suited for our desires and present abilities. It is an optional path we alone define by our very behavior in the present.[51]

The inhabitants of celestial and infernal regions are clairvoyant and telepathic by birth. These abilities do not arise from the dissolution of karma, but are a fundamental feature of their current level of existence. Any karma that might block extrasensory perception on the human level of existence becomes inactive during the time spent in celestial or infernal regions.

Though the ability is inborn, *devas* and *narakas* do not all possess the same degree of clairvoyance. The differences mirror their individual degrees of development. As human beings perceive true or flawed knowledge through their senses, *devas* and *narakas* also take in true or flawed knowledge through clairvoyance.

---

51 We get a taste of the mechanics of these two regions in our dreams. Here our desires and thoughts manifest instantly - the ones we *want* to experience as well as those we *dread*. We remain immersed in a particular sequence of events for as long as our desire binds our consciousness to its inner content. Only by extracting our attention from this content - i.e. when we rise above our desires that attracted the event - do we become able to leave situations we are entangled in.

Time is of hardly any issue here - we may feel immersed in a particular dream for years, yet when we wake up in this reality, mere 20 minutes may have passed. Our 'dream-body' appears indestructible and its form quite changeable. And we seem to confront *everything* we missed or were able to avoid in this reality.

SUTRA 22

क्षयोपशमनिमित्तः षड्विकल्पः शेषाणाम् ॥ २२ ॥

Kshayopashama nimittah sadvikalpah shesanam (22)

Human beings and animals experience six types of extrasensory perception (*avadhi*) once their respective karmas are dissolved. (22)

Extrasensory perception is blocked by several types of karma. The strongest block totally prevents access to this channel. The weaker blocks interfere with the clarity with which we experience clairvoyant and telepathic activities.

We begin to perceive the world beyond our senses when the respective karmic bonds are either <u>completely</u> dissolved or become <u>temporarily inactive</u>. In the second case we experience clairvoyance for some time, but lose it again.

Extrasensory abilities arise when we dissolve the prejudices and misconceptions (our karmas) that obstruct this type of perception - and by recognizing and amplifying this special sensation each time it occurs. Once we orient towards growth, we automatically activate factors that advance our clairvoyant and telepathic abilities.

Since *devas* and *narakas* experience clairvoyance by birth, the sutra emphasizes that human beings can acquire this ability only <u>by their own efforts</u>.

Extrasensory perception occurs in six variations:

1 - <u>Accompanying</u> (*anugami*) - We take our ability to use this channel with us when we move to another place or from one incarnation to the next.

2 - <u>Fleeting</u> (*ananugami*) - We lose this kind of perception once place or circumstances change.

3 - Growing (*vardhamana*) - We recognize ever more subtle areas of life. Our ability develops in the same degree in which we advance our orientation towards growth. The expansion of our perception is not limited.

4 - Decreasing (*hiyamana*) - Our ability declines in the same degree as our orientation towards growth decreases. The regions we cognize are more and more reduced until we perceive (almost) nothing beyond our senses.

5 - Steady (*avasthita*) Our extrasensory abilities neither increase nor decrease. They continue in the intensity and range in which they emerged. Their scope and steadiness mirror the stability and intensity of our orientation towards growth.

6 - Changeable (*anavasthita*) - Our insight into the world beyond the senses is as unsteady as a wave moved by the wind. It increases and deteriorates in the same degree as our orientation towards growth increases or declines.

Through extrasensory perception we receive true as well as erroneous information.

In our last incarnation before reaching ultimate freedom (*moksa*), the fleeting, decreasing and changeable varieties of extrasensory perception cease to arise.

SUTRA 23

ऋजुविपुलमती मनःपर्ययः ॥ २३ ॥

Rjuvipulamati manahparyayah (23)

Direct perception of the consciousness of others (*manah-paryaya*) occurs in two intensities:

- **in simple form (*rijumati*) and**
- **as deep, comprehensive insight (*vipulamati*). (23)**

Direct mental perception (*manah-paryaya*) is a state of consciousness where we sense the degree of realization of another person directly in our own consciousness. Once this channel activates, the boundaries that normally exist between the consciousness of two people fall away. Any communication through external means (words, gestures etc.) becomes irrelevant during this period, and distance in space ceases to be an obstruction.

Direct mental perception is an excellent means of transferring multilayered insights in a highly precise way. It is not subject to error and misunderstanding.

The scope and depth of the perceived insights mirrors the degree to which <u>our</u> consciousness already opened to higher levels of perception (even if we are not fully aware of it).

Direct mental perception rises gradually as the karmas that blocked its activation either dissolve or become inactive (latent).

- **The simple form** (*rijumati*) cognizes insights that reach up to eight incarnations into the future and past - of ourselves and others. It gives us insight into future and past incarnations.

  Simple direct knowledge works up to a distance of about 12 km, but not beyond it.

- **Deep, comprehensive direct perception** (*vipulamati*) is not limited by time.

  It encompasses the entire range where human beings reside, but does not reach beyond this boundary.

S U T R A   2 4

विशुद्धय प्रतिपाताभ्यां तद्विशेषः ॥ २४ ॥

Vishuddhya pratipatabhyam tadvishesah (24)

These two types of direct mental perception (*manah-paryaya*) differ in their degree of clarity and in the possibility of losing this ability again. (24)

We experience direct mental perception (*manah-paryaya*) from the seventh to the twelfth stage of development.

Two factors determine the degree in which direct mental perception manifests:

- **The clarity of what we directly perceive** is determined by the degree to which the respective blocking karma has been dissolved or became inactive.

    Comprehensive direct perception (*vipulamati*) is far clearer than its simple form (*rjumati*). It recognizes far subtler forms of matter and higher dimensions of reality than is accessible to the simple variation.

- **The possibility of losing this ability again** depends on which of two paths we choose in the seventh stage of development[52] (*apramatta virata*).

    1 - *The suspension of karma.* On this path most our remaining karma recedes into a latent, inactive state. Since up to stage eleven inactive karma does not obstruct progress, this enables us to experience the character of the higher stages. The path leads via level 8, 9 and 10 to level 11, from where we go back to any of the lower levels.

    Our ascent beyond level 11 is blocked as long as our emotional longing for experiences on lower levels - (our latent, inactive karma) - obstructs further advancement.

    As long as we do *not fundamentally dissolve* our remaining karma, we only get access to the *simple* form (*rjumati*) of this channel.

---

52 see '14 STAGES OF DEVELOPMENT' - stage seven

2 - *The dissolution of karma* - Here we dissolve our remaining karma once and for all. On this path we bypass level 11 and ascend via stage 8, 9, 10, 12, 13 to stage 14 and then to liberation. This path is the only way to liberation.

The second, more comprehensive and far superior intensity of direct perception (*vipulamati*) activates instantly once we begin to *fundamentally dissolve* our inclination to experience the lower stages of development (our remaining karma).

The ascent from stage 7 to stage 11 cannot be compared to any of the mechanisms we encounter in stage 1 to 4. Most people remain for a long time in stage 1 to 4 and regard any advance to higher stages as exceptional, arduous and difficult.

Yet as soon as we reach the fifth stage of development, the unfoldment of our consciousness accelerates considerably. Since some of the more advanced stages permit only a short duration of stay, continuous change is foreordained. We now regard the shift from one stage to another as something natural and comfortable.

Our frequent ascent from stage 7 to stage 11 can be compared to practicing an approach run in sports. Like in training high jump, we prepare to take the last hurdle before the full unfoldment of our consciousness.

But the decision to dissolve *all* our remaining karma instead of just choosing its mere *suspension* is not easy. Though in stage 7 we clearly decided to go for ultimate freedom, subtle emotional tendencies still attach us to this world. As long as we are unwilling to depart the narrow experiences of the lower levels we completed long ago, we block ourselves from again assuming our majestic, unlimited self.

It is essential to understand that it is *entirely OUR OWN decision when* to dissolve our final bonds, - i.e. when to choose the second path that inevitably leads to ultimate freedom.

SUTRA 25

विशुद्धिक्षेत्रस्वामिविषयेभ्योऽवधिमनःपर्यययोः ॥ २५ ॥

Vishuddhikshetrasvamivisayebhyoavadhimanahparyayayoh (25)

Direct mental perception (*manah-paryaya*) differs from extrasensory perception (*avadhi*) by

- its clarity
- the spatial boundaries in which it functions
- the degree of realization of the perceiver and
- the type of the perceived objects. (25)

Both - clairvoyance/telepathy and direct mental perception - reach into regions beyond the range of the five senses. Yet apart from this common feature these two channels differ significantly from each other.

1 - **Clarity** - Direct mental perception cognizes its objects far clearer than clairvoyance and telepathy. It can penetrate into subtle and subtlest aspects while clairvoyance and telepathy perceive only gross levels in comparison.

2 - **The spatial boundaries in which they function** - Clairvoyance and telepathy extend to the entire universe while direct mental perception covers only the range where human beings reside.

Though the space in which direct mental perception functions is limited, it cognizes *qualitatively* far subtler dimensions than clairvoyance and telepathy.

3 - **The degree of realization of the perceiver** - Clairvoyance and telepathy can be obtained by all beings in possession of a mind - i.e. human beings, *devas* and *narakas*.

Direct mental perception arises only in human beings in the seventh to twelfth stage of development.

4 - **The type of the perceived objects** - Clairvoyance and telepathy perceive all elements (living beings, matter, space, time etc.), but not all their features (e.g. their more subtle manifestations).

Direct mental perception only cognizes *contents present in the consciousness of others*. Yet it is capable of taking in even the subtlest insights others have realized in their life and integrated into their consciousness. Direct mental perception enables us to use the accumulated wisdom of another person as if it were our own. To what depth we perceive this depends exclusively on *our own* degree of realization.

While clairvoyance and telepathy work with the help of the mind, direct mental perception uses the mind only like a projection-screen of a movie theatre that enables the perception of a movie. The screen does not influence the original message of the movie, but the screen's quality may alter the clarity of what we perceive. In a similar way our mind mirrors the degree of *our* realization and thus determines to what depth we are able to perceive the other consciousness.

SUTRA 26

मतिश्रुतयोर्निबन्धो द्रव्येष्वसर्वपर्यायेषु ॥ २६ ॥

Matishrutayor nibandho dravyesva sarva paryayesu (26)

Sense-perception and external knowledge perceive all six elements (living beings, matter, time etc.), but not all their features. (26)

Sense-perception (*mati*) and scriptural knowledge (*sruti*) have access to only a limited range of the infinite multitude of features, forms and aspects the six elements can manifest. These two channels e.g.

do not perceive our interactive karmic field that consists of karmic matter (subtle molecules) and surrounds us permanently.[53]

SUTRA 27

रूपिष्ववधेः ॥ २७ ॥

Rupisvavadheh (27)

Extrasensory perception (*avadhi*) perceives all that has form, but not all its features. (27)

Extrasensory perception (clairvoyance, telepathy etc.) is limited to the range of matter (*pudgala*). This channel does _not_ perceive any of the _non-material_ elements. Though it perceives _subtle_ forms, it is unable to recognize _all_ forms matter can assume.

---

53 The space our body occupies contains an infinite number of karmic molecules. These molecules operate in a different range than the molecules of matter and are also far smaller. They cannot be directly perceived by our senses.

If - by our inclinations and intentions - we stimulate a (limited) number of these karmic molecules, they either cause immediate activity or attach to our interactive karmic field in a latent form to manifest activity at a later point in time. Without this stimulation by our intention and activity - that connect our consciousness (*jiva*) to karmic matter (*ajiva*) - karmic molecules have no effect, even if they take up the same space as our body.

Those karmic molecules attached to our interactive karmic field remain only within the limits of the bodies we inhabit during incarnations. Apart from manifesting activity they have no further function. Individual karma is _not_ stored _outside_ our bodily form.

The activation of karmic molecules brings their latent energy into a form we can experience. Activation totally dissolves the bond between our consciousness and the manifested karmic molecules. After they manifested activity, the corresponding karmic molecules cease to influence our life.

SUTRA 28

तदनन्तभागे मनःपर्ययस्य ॥ २८ ॥

Tadananta bhage manahparyayasya (28)

Direct mental perception (*manah-paryaya*) perceives far subtler forms than extrasensory perception (*avadhi*). (28)

Even the highest form of extrasensory perception (clairvoyance, telepathy etc.) does not reach into the subtle areas direct perception of the consciousness of others can access.

Yet the deepest direct mental perception does not perceive *the entire multitude* of all possible manifestations. The stage of development where direct mental perception activates is not stable enough for experiencing omniscience.

SUTRA 29

सर्वद्रव्यपर्यायेषु केवलस्य ॥ २९ ॥

Sarva dravya paryayesu kevalasya (29)

Omniscience (*kevala jnana*) perceives all elements and all their manifestations simultaneously. (29)

Omniscience perceives all elements and all their features and manifestations in the present, past and future simultaneously.

Omniscience arises automatically when our consciousness is not restricted by deluding karma any more. Though we may still have other karmic bonds, they cease to effect the vastness of our consciousness. Once we reached omniscience, we never lose it again.

We experience *full* omniscience as soon as it arises for the first time. There are no different degrees of omniscience.

We do _not_ experience omniscience _through our mind_, because the mind cannot direct its attention to a multitude of _simultaneous_ events and objects.

Omniscience is not caused by any external means; - it is the complete unfoldment of our consciousness by itself.

As soon as we reach omniscience, we cease to experience the other four types of knowledge. We remain subject to them only as long as our consciousness is limited by karma.

As long as we are influenced by _time_ (_kala_), we experience the world as a chain of events that lead us to ever deeper and more comprehensive insights. While in the first twelve stages of development, new insights therefore appear to us like the end-result of a sequence of events.

Yet a _time of emergence_ of an insight only exists in those stages of development that are _below_ omniscience. In the state of omniscience our consciousness _ceases to be influenced by time_. Concepts like 'consecutive', simultaneous' or 'sequence' do not apply any more and there is no 'evolution' of insights as we know it presently.

Here ends the description of the range and character of knowledge - i.e. which regions of our consciousness the five channels give us access to.

SUTRA 30

एकादीनि भाज्यानि युगपदेकस्मिन्नाचतुर्भ्यः ॥ ३० ॥

Ekadini bhajyani yugapade kasminna chaturbhyah (30)

One up to four channels of knowledge can be active simultaneously. (30)

We can experience one up to four channels of knowledge simultaneously, but never more than four.

- **One** channel of knowledge. - In the state of omniscience (*kevala jnana*) we experience only this <u>one</u> - all-comprehensive - channel.

Omniscience is characterized by the <u>*absence of karmic bonds*</u>. Since the other four channels function only when our consciousness is limited by karma, they cannot operate simultaneously with omniscience.

Once we gained omniscience, we also have no need to experience knowledge through less perfect channels.

- **Two** simultaneously active channels of knowledge are sense-perception (*mati*) and external knowledge (*sruti*). All human beings - except the omniscient - have access to at least these two types of knowledge.

- **Three** simultaneously active channels of knowledge are either

    - sense-perception (*mati*), external knowledge (*sruti*) and extrasensory perception (*avadhi*), or

    - sense-perception (*mati*), external knowledge (*sruti*) and direct mental perception (*manah-paryaya*).

Since external knowledge is perceived by sense-perception first, these two channels need to be active simultaneously - irrespective of the third channel we use.

- **Four** simultaneously active channels of knowledge are

    - sense-perception (*mati*)
    - external knowledge (*sruti*)
    - extrasensory perception (*avadhi*) and
    - direct mental perception (*manah-paryaya*).

SUTRA 31

मतिश्रुतावधयो विपर्ययश्च ॥ ३१ ॥

Mati shruta vadhayo viparyayashcha (31)

- Sense-perception (*mati*)
- knowledge from external sources (*sruti*) and
- clairvoyance (*avadhi*)

can also produce error. (31)

What causes error?

We experience error when we project concepts onto our perception that do not correspond with reality.

We experience error, when we cease to orient towards growth and thus forego our flawless intuitive insight into reality.

The cause for error is <u>not</u> the process of perception. When we orient towards growth, we perceive exactly the same forms, colors etc. as someone subjected to erroneous concepts. Error is caused when we do not orient <u>the processing</u> of our perception towards the purpose of reality (see sutra 2).

Error manifests in form of

- <u>Doubt, skepticism, uncertainty</u> (*samshaya*) - Doubt and skepticism <u>reject</u> insights how to re-orient our ideas and actions before they can stimulate us. Even though we recognize these (temporary) insights more or less clearly, we refuse this offer to change our perspectives and action-patterns. Doubt and skepticism always express inner uncertainty.

  We either acquire (learn) doubt and skepticism from 'role-models' we imitate, or give in to outside pressure not to violate conventional opinions and behavior, or by accepting established patterns and taboos out of social opportunism.

- <u>Confusion of truth</u> (*viparyaya*) - is the firm conviction that our own concepts are right, even if they do not correspond with reality.

  Concepts based on flawed assumptions often appear surprisingly logical. As long as our thinking remains trapped in such models, it is impossible to discover the flaws in their construction. Without challenging the model from an *outside* perspective, our awareness will stay within the limits of the erroneous concept.

  Adhering to a flawed concept often has the psychological effect that we subconsciously check all our experiences and events whether they fit into our cherished model. Facts that do not agree with the presumed concept are ignored, interpreted as unimportant, forgotten or not even perceived - *without us being able to control this process*.

- <u>Carelessness, indifference, confusion</u> (*anadhayavasaya*)

  <u>Carelessness</u> is a lack of interest in everything that could further our inner growth. *All* negligence towards any person or object always also indicates a lack of respect *towards ourselves*.

  <u>Indifference</u> is the tendency not to end a state of error and flawed concepts though we receive some (temporary) insight into the true mechanisms of this world. We feel an impulse to reevaluate our habitual behavior or to try out new types of action, but decline to follow this impulse because of laziness.

  Carelessness and indifference - no matter towards whom or what - block inner growth. We only gain conscious and stable access to superior levels of consciousness if we commit *the best* of our energies and abilities towards this goal.

  <u>Confusion</u> often mistakes cause and effect or assumes wrong causes. Many believe e.g. that passion is caused by matter (e.g. that it arises when we perceive a coveted object or person). In

reality passion is caused within ourselves (by our own thoughts and emotions) and then projected onto an object of desire.

Error is caused

- from within ourselves or
- by the influence of others - i.e. when we accept (believe in) concepts, teachings and belief-systems based on error.

Both variations block our ability to find the way to more satisfying and comprehensive levels of inner growth.

Objection: We cannot possibly *always* orient our life towards growth so that we always recognize true knowledge. To achieve this our consciousness and senses would need to be flawless and working perfectly. Short of reaching total freedom from karma this is impossible.

Furthermore - why should someone who is *not* growth-oriented not also receive true knowledge at some time or another, even if this insight does not last?

And finally - what about all those who discover unknown things e.g. in the realm of science and who achieve the same results as other researchers. Should this not be called 'gaining true knowledge'?

Answer: There are two kinds of beings: those (*bhavya*), who direct their life towards achieving freedom from karmic limitations, and those who mainly care about worldly life (*abhavya*).

All those who really aspire total freedom, possess a special sense of discrimination: they know intuitively what knowledge and what lines of action will bring them closer to their goal. They attain the ability to arrange the components of their life in such a way that it supports the unfolding of consciousness.

All those *not* aspiring this freedom, concentrate mainly on the material range of reality (sometimes on its more subtle aspects like art etc.). But as intelligent, clear and comprehensive the knowledge and perception of such person may appear, they are and will remain temporary and do not contribute to inner growth. Each so-called progress is accidental and unstable.[54]

The next sutra continues to answer the objection:

SUTRA 32

सदसतोरविशेषाद्यदृच्छोपलब्धेरुन्मत्तवत् ॥ ३२ ॥

Sadasato ravishesadya drichchhopa labdhe runmattavat (32)

Someone trapped in error does not discriminate between the real and the unreal. Like a lunatic he assigns meaning to objects and events that is subjected to his constantly changing moods. (32)

A lunatic who sometimes sees things clearly and calls them by their right name, is far from able to discriminate between right and wrong on a *permanent* basis. All his knowledge - even if he gets it right at times - is *fundamentally* flawed.

All those who focus their attention on material life are in a similar situation. No matter how comprehensive and refined their knowledge may appear, from the perspective of reaching ultimate freedom

---

[54] *We ourselves* decide to which class of beings we belong. We either develop our potential abilities available to *all* beings, or we don't. We are *bhavya* when we orient towards growth and actively unfold our consciousness. If we do *not* to follow this direction, we consequently will not reach total freedom (*abhavya*).

All *abhavyas* foolishly confuse 'potential' and 'realization'. They pacify themselves with the suggestion that they *COULD start any time*. Yet a huge gap exists between potential and its realization. Of everything we do *not* do *now* - in the present, - we never know if we will ever do it 'later', or if conducive circumstances will ever occur again. - We also do not know if in our last 10.000 incarnations we haven't left this for tomorrow as well, - and then wonder, why 'this' life is not turning out as we desire. If we decide for procrastination *now*, we program ourselves to procrastinate in future as well.

they have no insight into the nature of their consciousness. None of their (materially oriented) knowledge stimulates the unfoldment of their inherent potential.

The amount of worldly knowledge or material possessions have absolutely no effect on our spiritual development. _Orientation towards inner growth_ is the decisive factor that arranges all our knowledge - how little it may be - in such a way that it leads us to ever more comprehensive insights into higher dimensions of our life.

* * *

Here ends the description of Total Perception - _pramana_.

The next sutra explains the mechanism of partial sight - _naya_.

S U T R A   3 3

नैगमसंग्रह व्यवहार र्जुसूत्रशब्दसमभिरूढैवंभूता नयाः ॥ ३३ ॥

Naigama sangraha vayvahara rjusutra shabda samabhirud-haivambhuta nayah (33)

Knowledge from partial sight (_naya_) is gained in seven steps:

   1 - outlining an indistinct experience (_naigama_)

   2 - recognizing the interconnected whole behind the experience (_sangraha_)

   3 - identifying its functional elements (_vyavahara_)

   4 - asserting what really manifests in the present (_rju sutra_)

   5 - deepening the insight by verbally describing it (_sabda_)

   6 - condensing this conscious insight into _one_ clear image (_samabhirudha_)

   7 - integrating this one clear image into our consciousness (_evambhuta_). (33)

Partial sight (*naya*) - is a systematic method to gain knowledge of _one_ _particular aspect_ of reality. With the technique of partial sight we examine conditions or features of objects and events _from one particular_ _perspective_ only.

Partial sight focuses our attention on _one_ specific aspect of reality like looking at it through a magnifying glass.

The deeper and the more precise we penetrate a partial aspect, the deeper and clearer will be our comprehension of the _entire level of re-_ _ality_ of which this aspect is a part. Profound insight into _one single_ _experience_ may thus open our understanding for an entire level of reality - as the part often reveals the whole behind it.[55]

The sutra introduces a systematic method for exploring partial areas of our reality. It describes seven _consecutive and interdependent_ steps that lead us ever closer to the examined object. The last step is the full integration of the (new) insight into our consciousness. Like in Total Perception - *pramana* - the insight then becomes part of the basis of integrated knowledge we rely on for steering our life.

The method of partial sight is exquisitely suited for becoming aware of vague experiences. It works even faster when we use it in dialogue with similarly interested people. It is much easier to verbalize our insights - step 5 - if we have a partner to talk to.

Since reality is a complex object, there of course exists an infinite number of partial views (*nayas*) from which this object (reality) can be perceived. The Tattvarthasutra states that _every_ perspective - as global as it might appear - always only represents a _partial truth_. The

---

[55] Though the expansion of understanding from part to the whole happens on intuitive levels beyond intellectual patterns like logic or deduction, it is not less precise and systematic. We experience insights of this kind as sudden dynamic understanding, where our mind and feelings encounter an intuitive rearrangement of meaning. _All_ new ideas, concepts, inventions etc. this world ever produced originated in this kind of dynamic insight.

work accepts fundamentally that _other_ perspectives and partial truths - different from its own - may be equally valid.

This understanding is the basis of a sovereign tolerance towards differing views, opinions, religions and philosophies that looks for its equal. The fundamental recognition that _we_ cannot possibly comprehend reality in its entirety[56], makes us understand that _others_ can also only see and interpret the world from _their_ particular angle. They voice their views with exactly _the same legitimacy_ we assume for our own positions.

This sovereignty and tolerance make us realize how many philosophies interpret the world from only _one_ particular point of view while at the same time demanding absolute and universal validity for their partial perspective.[57]

Tolerance towards the partial views of others allows us to accept that even _contradictory_ perspectives might well be in harmony with each other if we only regard them as _different aspects of one and the same reality_.

Yet partial sight (_naya_) is far more than a precise analytical instrument. The seven steps do not only help us to examine and broaden new insights, or to arrange reality in such a systematic way that its infinite variety can be more easily understood. The seven steps stimulate us to search for ever more subtle and more fundamental levels of understanding and this inevitably opens our consciousness to broader regions of reality.

---

56 except in the state of omniscience

57 This ambition often leads to the exclusion of extensive parts of reality. The missing parts are usually either plainly ignored or substituted by dogmatic beliefs that do not permit questioning. Philosophies or belief-systems with this kind of ambition therefore hardly ever agree with the _unrestricted and independent_ development of our full potential.

Partial sight (*naya*) generates knowledge in seven steps:

1 - Outlining an experience (*naigama*)

By outlining an experience we mark one part of reality without clearly defining it. We do not bother about details we might not perceive distinctly (yet). By outlining an experience we separate it from 'the rest of reality' and make it tangible enough for us to analyze it.

EXAMPLE: We perceive a new object. Something inside the object is ringing. If we speak to the object in a certain way, it answers.

'There is something interesting.'

2 - Recognizing the interconnected whole behind the experience (*sangraha*)

Here we shift our attention to the fundamental whole beyond the individual details we perceived in step one.

We consciously withdraw our energy from perceiving details. We focus instead on finding the meaning behind it and try to discover a coherent whole in all the many parts. This attempt, this energy we *consciously focus* is the crucial factor that ultimately enables us to identify the underlying whole.

EXAMPLE: We ask friends what the object might be. We understand eventually that this is a method to talk to people who are not within hearing distance.

'What is it exactly?'

It is essential to understand that we do not have to experience *all details* first before we receive an impression of the whole.

3 - Identifying its functional elements (*vyavahara*)

After we determined what the fundamental whole is, we now try to recognize its structure and its parts, - we identify its functional elements.

EXAMPLE: We find out that a cable connects a receiver to the object. We understand that there are keys through which we can input numbers that cause similar objects in other places to become active.

'How does it work?'

Vyavahara is the primary mechanism that shapes our _present_ perception of reality. - In its current state of karmic limitation our consciousness splits the totality of this universe into small parts and single action-sequences. Our present state of embodiment makes us perceive these single events in great detail and like in slow motion so we can physically experience how certain features of this universe work.

4 - Asserting what really manifests in the present (*rju sutra*).

The PRESENT is the only time that gives us access to reality.

Everything we do, everything we experience, everything that confronts us, only happens in the present. Even if we think of the past (when we remember something), or plan the future, we do this only in the present. Therefore only what we experience here and now can give us information about an object, an event, or ourselves.

But in the present we experience not only mere temporary, fleeting manifestations. _Fleetingness_ is only _one_ aspect of the present. Every object or event - irrespective how fleeting it may be - always also mirrors the _totality of the reality_ that caused it to manifest.

The statement 'I am happy' e.g. describes a positive experience in the present. The basis of this statement - the being that is cheerful, the cause and the type of its joy etc. are implied without needing to be specifically mentioned.

All events that happen in the present also express everything that brought about their appearance. Origin, content, emotions, associations, projections, concepts, - all this resonates within us as well while we observe an event. That we are mostly unaware of this is simply because _we never put our attention_ on this _comprehensive_ aspect of the present and the immense potential insight it offers us.

In the Western hemisphere we focus mainly on the _fleeting_ aspect of the present. We see time as a line that comes from an infinite past and runs into an equally infinite future. In these seemingly gigantic masses of past and future the present takes up such a minute point, it seems almost a miracle that we perceive it at all.

Yet this again is only a concept. It is only _our very idea of time_ that produces this _devaluation of the present_. We arbitrarily take that part of the present we _feel familiar with_ and define it as 'the past'. We take _our expectations and hopes_ and define it as 'the future'. The little that remains we either assign to the present or discard it because we don't know where to put it. It is _only this concept_ that makes us regard past and future as so important and domineering that we allow them to overshadow major sections of our present.[58]

We forget that _only the present_ can give us access to _everything_. We neglect that behind its characteristic fleetingness we also perceive all the 'invisible' influences that led to the manifestation of a specific event or form in the first place.

---

[58] We even define _ourselves_ on the basis of our past. We take bygone experiences and project them into our future. We regard events as inevitable only because we are familiar with the way they happened in the past and because we want to believe that they would do the same in the future.

The statement e.g. 'I am unhappy (now)' describes a negative experience in the present. The experience might be over in a second. Yet how often do we feel 'I will continue to be unhappy in all future' though we do not know the future and though all our circumstances may change at any moment.

In this fourth step we therefore examine how an object or event manifests in our present and how this actual manifestation mirrors its underlying 'durable' and comprehensive reality.

EXAMPLE: We purchase a telephone and talk to friends, relatives and other people who live far away.

We notice that this makes it easy to coordinate future events with others, that we receive information very fast etc. We eventually observe that the possibility of fast and easy communication (by telephone) significantly changes our life. We recognize that the machine's influence extends far beyond the content of any individual telephone call - as important as it may be.

'What do we really experience now?'

We are not interested in theoretical knowledge that may influence us in some future time, but only in the real effect we experience in the present - but this in all its depth.[59]

5 - Deepening the insight by verbally describing it (*sabda*)

After we found out what really effects us, we intensify this experience by verbalizing it.

EXAMPLE: We tell others how the telephone works and what kind of opportunities it offers. This makes us more aware of our relationship with the machine and the effect is has on our life.

'How can it be described?'

One of the best methods to make us more aware of an insight is to express it in words. This process moves the insight right into the center of our awareness.

---

[59] Only the present is able to connect us to the entire, rich foundation of an event. Only the immediate present gives us access to the entire reality an experience is made up of.

Memories of past events always cover only a small spectrum of what really happened - and this spectrum gets even smaller the more removed an event is. What part of the past we are able to remember is further influenced heavily by our current mood and situation.

6 - Condensing this conscious insight into *one* clear image (*samabhirudha*)

The previous step made us aware of the insight we had. We now condense this insight into <u>one</u> clear picture.

EXAMPLE: We combine all individual aspects of the telephone into <u>one</u> single experience. We do not separate the individual components any more, but condense the entire complex mechanism of telephone-communication and all the possibilities it offers into <u>*one characteristic experience*</u>.

We also experience this when we are reading. We condense letters, words and sentences in such a way that on a higher level we perceive a <u>*comprehensive*</u> meaning that goes far beyond the range of single words or sentences.

'Yes, that's it!'

7 - Integrating this one clear image into our consciousness (*evambhuta*)

In step six we are still separated from our insight. Certainly - we acquired an ability, an expertise, assured knowledge, - but its application still requires special attention.

In this seventh step we fully integrate the condensed experience into our life so that it ceases to be separate from us. From now onwards we apply it without needing to raise special attention or energy for this purpose.

EXAMPLE: We regard fast communication to all points of the globe as a foundation of our life, - as normal as reading, speaking etc. We use this ability so automatically and comfortably that we put our attention only on the <u>*content*</u> we intend to communicate, but hardly ever think about the technical processes that make it possible.

Another example is driving. After we trained the ability and practiced it for a while, we never waste a thought on the mechanics. We sit behind the steering-wheel and think about where we want to go, what to do when we arrive etc., but never how all the levers and switches operate inside or how the engine works.

'Let's apply it.'

This integration of (new) insights into our consciousness happens automatically when we discard all mental concepts, contents and emotions that we projected onto the experience *while developing or training* it, but that have nothing to do with the actual insight itself.

Driving a car becomes a natural ability when we stop thinking how much we liked or disliked our driving teacher, how expensive it was to get the license or what we felt during the theoretical test. Once all superfluous content is discarded we only manifest the pure ability. Our new insight or ability has now become an integrated and effortless part of our consciousness.

The seven steps are far more complex than can be described in this book. They also constitute one part of a comprehensive system of logic that developed over the last millennium and on which voluminous books were written. Whoever likes to ponder elaborate theoretical arguments should consider reading these works.

Yet our very own, direct experience is and remains the best key to new insights. Therefore this book mainly concentrated on opening *practical access* to this knowledge so that everyone may understand and apply it without outside assistance.

We only experience the path to ultimate freedom by *progressing on the path itself*, - never by the mere reading of books or by any kind of *preliminary training* that only moves our start further and further into the future and carries the danger of losing ourselves in endless, superfluous preparation.

The path to ultimate freedom exists - but only to the extent *WE begin with it*.

TEXT OF THE SUTRAS

THE KEY TO THE
CENTER OF THE UNIVERSE

(Chapter 1 of the Tattvarthasutra)

(1)   - The intuition how to optimally unfold our consciousness
       (*samyag darshana*)
       - knowledge that makes us recognize and understand this un-
       folding of consciousness (*samyag jnana*) and
       - the manifestation of these insights in action (*samyag charitra*)
       are the path to liberation.

(2) Confidence in the purpose of reality is the origin of our intuitive
    orientation towards growth.

(3) Confidence in the purpose of reality and orientation towards
    growth (*samyag darshana*) arise either
       - intuitively (*nisarga*) or
       - when we acquire a special kind of knowledge (*adhigama*).

(4)   - The individual impulse of life - '_that what lives_ in a living being' - (_jiva_)

- the elements that do _not_ possess consciousness (_ajiva_)

- the mechanism that _attracts_ karmic matter to our consciousness (_asrava_)

- the _binding_ of karmic matter to our consciousness (_bandha_)

- the _termination_ of the process that binds karmic matter to our life (_samvara_)

- the _separation_ of karmic matter from our consciousness (_nirjara_) and

- _freedom_ from all influences that limit our innate qualities and abilities (_moksa_)

are reality.

(5) We experience reality (consciousness, matter, time etc.) on four different planes:

- on the plane of names - where we use names and terms for the purpose of communication and social mechanisms (_nama_)

- on the plane of selection - where we filter our individual reality from the constant barrage of billions of inner and outer stimuli (_sthapana_)

- on the plane of all potentially possible features of the elements - which constitutes the basis for the identical perception of reality by different people (_dravya_) and

- on the plane of facts - where individual features of the elements (or a combination of them) influence our actual present (_bhava_).

(6) We obtain insight into reality either

- by *Total Perception* (*pramana*), where we comprehend the *totality* of the appearance of the elements (i.e. their forms, features and interactions) as they manifest in the present, or

- through *partial sight* (*naya*), where we perceive manifestations of the elements from a *limited perspective*.

(7) We develop Total Perception - *pramana* - by

- directing our attention towards this particular ability of our consciousness (*nirdesha*)

- by recognizing and accepting the insights we gain as our own (*svamitva*)

- by becoming aware of its mechanisms and features (*sadhana*)

- by discovering what causes it to arise (*adhikarana*)

- by consciously prolonging its duration (*sthiti*) and

- by allowing Total Perception to influence our life (*vidhana*).

(8) Total Perception - *pramana* - perceives

- the existence (*sat*)

- the features and functions (*sankhya*)

- the place of manifestation (*kshetra*)

- the immediate sense-experience (*sparshana*)

- the time and duration of manifestation (*kala*)

- the inner purpose and meaning (*antara*)

- the presently active features (*bhava*)

- the extent, quantities and proportions (*alpa-bahutva*)

of all six elements and their manifestations.

(9) We access knowledge (*jnana*) through five different channels:
- our senses (*mati*)
- external sources (scriptures, teachers etc.) (*sruti*)
- extrasensory perception (clairvoyance, telepathy etc.) (*avadhi*)
- direct perception of the consciousness of others (*manah-paryaya*) and
- omniscience (*kevala jnana*).

(10) All five channels of knowledge operate with Total Perception - *pramana*.

(11) The first two channels give us *indirect* access to knowledge.

(12) The remaining three channels provide *direct* access to knowledge.

(13) - Recollection (of something known before, but presently not in contact with our senses) (*smrtih*)
- recognition (of an object known before, when the object itself or something similar or markedly dissimilar is presented to our senses) (*sanjna*)
- induction (reasoning on the basis of observation) (*chinta*)
- deduction (reasoning by inference) (*abhinibodha*)

are also considered sensory knowledge (*mati*).

(14) Sensory knowledge (*mati*) is triggered by our senses *and the mind*.

(15) Sensory knowledge develops in four stages:

    1 - apprehension (*avagraha*)

    2 - forming a first idea of what we perceived (*iha*)

    3 - evaluation of our perception (*avaya*)

    4 - consolidating and storing the perception and its evaluation in our memory (*dharana*).

(16) Sense-perception recognizes twelve fundamental features of the perceived objects and events:

    1 - many (*bahu*)

    2 - few (one unit) (*eka*)

    3 - many kinds (*bahuvidha*)

    4 - few kinds (one kind) (*ekavidha*)

    5 - fast (*ksipra*)

    6 - slow (*aksipra*)

    7 - partial (*anihsrita*)

    8 - complete (*nihsrita*)

    9 - perceived indirectly (*anukta*)

    10 - perceived directly (*ukta*)

    11 - steady, permanent (*dhruva*)

    12 - transient (*adhruva*).

(17) Sense-perception (*mati*) perceives not only the outer (visible) characteristics of an element, but its entire content, purpose and meaning.

(18) The first step of sense-perception - apprehension (*avagraha*) - perceives objects and events in an _indistinct_ way.

(19) Indistinct apprehension does not arise through the eyes or the mind.

(20) Knowledge we obtain from external sources (*sruti*) first needs to be perceived by our senses.

There are two types of scriptures. The first type has twelve, the second one many divisions.

(21) In the inhabitants of celestial and nether regions extrasensory perception (*avadhi*) is inborn.

(22) Human beings and animals experience six types of extrasensory perception (*avadhi*) once their respective karmas are dissolved.

(23) Direct perception of the consciousness of others (*manah-paryaya*) occurs in two intensities:

- in simple form (*rjumati*) and

- as deep, comprehensive insight (*vipulamati*).

(24) These two types of direct mental perception (*manah-paryaya*) differ in their degree of clarity and in the possibility of losing this ability again.

(25) Direct mental perception (*manah-paryaya*) differs from extrasensory perception (*avadhi*) by

- its clarity

- the spatial boundaries in which it functions

- the degree of realization of the perceiver and

- the type of the perceived objects.

(26) Sense-perception and external knowledge perceive all six elements (living beings, matter, time etc.), but not all their features.

(27) Extrasensory perception (*avadhi*) perceives all that has form, but not all its features.

(28) Direct mental perception (*manah-paryaya*) perceives far subtler forms than extrasensory perception (*avadhi*).

(29) Omniscience (*kevala jnana*) perceives all elements and all their manifestations simultaneously.

(30) One up to four channels of knowledge can be active simultaneously.

(31) - Sense-perception (*mati*)
      - knowledge from external sources (*sruti*) and
      - clairvoyance (*avadhi*)
      can also produce error.

(32) Someone trapped in error does not discriminate between the real and the unreal. Like a lunatic he assigns meaning to objects and events that is subjected to his constantly changing moods.

(33) Knowledge from partial sight (*naya*) is gained in seven steps:

     1 - outlining an indistinct experience (*naigama*)

     2 - recognizing the interconnected whole behind the experience (*sangraha*)

     3 - identifying its functional elements (*vyavahara*)

     4 - asserting what really manifests in the present (*rju sutra*)

     5 - deepening the insight by verbally describing it (*sabda*)

     6 - condensing this conscious insight into <u>one</u> clear image (*samabhirudha*)

     7 - integrating this one clear image into our consciousness (*evambhuta*).

APPLICATION

14 STAGES OF DEVELOPMENT

The Tattvarthasutra describes 14 stages (*gunasthanas*) human beings experience while striving for freedom from all karmic limitations. Each stage is characterized by the type of karma manifesting therein (what kind of emotions we feel, how intense they are and what types of action we experience as a result), the time we stay in one particular stage, the direction in which we pass through and how much our personal development is stimulated. Because of these differing factors each stage has a unique feeling and significance.

Our consciousness can be likened to a multi-story palace. The higher the floor, the more we see of the surrounding scenery. On the roof we have full view of the entire panorama and also unobstructed access to the sky. In the present situation of the world almost all people live in the basement that has no windows to the outside. Yet everyone is fully capable of living on any of the higher floors as well. The main reason for this restriction is that we don't know that higher levels exist.

This classification therefore enables us to identify our own present stage of development. Once we know its features and mechanisms, we are able to close all themes of life - dissolve all types of karma - that restrict us to our current level. We thus prevent wasting time and energy on efforts that would succeed only on higher levels.

Yet far more interesting is the fact that we often experience brief insights into 'higher' stages - irrespective of the level we presently reside in. Though the duration of these insights may be very short, they offer us a taste how higher levels feel like. These insights - however brief they may appear - prove vividly that _we are capable of experiencing the higher stages_. They tell us that it is well within our ability to reach entirely different layers of our consciousness and that we - only by re-directing our attention and energy - are capable of developing them into a permanent foundation of our life _now_.

Knowing the characteristics and mechanisms of the different _gunasthanas_ enables us to identify what level opened up when we have insights into higher stages.

In contrast to other systems of development the 14 _gunasthanas_ are not 'climbed' sequentially one after the other. We do not have to 'complete' one level first before we can progress to a higher one. The Tattvarthasutra describes an interconnected, complex structure that makes dynamic moves between distant stages an essential part of our development. The insights we obtain this way give us an immense incentive to wind up the themes of the lower levels so we can turn our attention towards exploring the far more fascinating higher stages.

We nevertheless should not judge higher stages as fundamentally 'better' than lower ones. In the end it is the experience of _all_ stages that makes up the fabric of our character we are building during bodily manifestations. While on a higher stage we might well decide that the - temporary - experience of a lower stage would be essential for our development and then consciously immerse ourselves into the greater emotional density and lesser comprehension of the lower stage for that very purpose.

Once we fundamentally understand how our consciousness unfolds, we never discount anyone who presently experiences a denser stage. We only feel profound compassion and appreciation for his or her particular path.

Only two *gunasthanas* (no. 1 and 4) permit an indefinite duration of stay. All other stages last for only a limited time. This structure gives the *gunasthanas* an intrinsic dynamism that coaxes us to gain freedom from all obstructions that restrict the full unfoldment of our consciousness.

1 - **We experience the first stage of development (*mithyaktva*)** as a state in which we are deeply absorbed by our convictions, emotions, our activities and by the events the world confronts us with.

Though we might think we fully control our life, any closer and deeper look reveals a drastically different picture:

- How often do we feel victimized by events we are hardly able to bear, let alone control?

- How often do we experience that any stability we worked so hard to achieve either breaks down in the end, - or solidifies our life so thoroughly that nothing is capable of moving us any more?

- How often are we really satisfied by the situation we are in or by the things we do and feel - and for how long does our satisfaction usually last?

- How often do our emotions tumble us from highest happiness to deepest misery (and vice versa) in one single second without us having much influence on this process?

- How often is our attention either arbitrarily drifting from object to object like a butterfly in the wind?

- How often are we so deeply absorbed by one particular concept, emotion or event that we hardly notice the world outside this dense envelope.

We might feel perfectly normal and clear in this environment, but this is only due to the fact that we know no alternate state that may introduce us to a different and more satisfying pattern of life. We live in a dense emotional cocoon we are hardly ever aware of. Though friends sometimes alert us to this condition, we have no idea how to get out of this almost hypnotic state. None of the goals we pursue on this level leads systematically to the experience of higher stages.

It is a state of delusion and flawed ideas how the world functions. All convictions, belief systems, viewpoints and opinions we found our life on retain us on this level - irrespective if we acquired them by our own efforts or accepted them from others. Even when presented with truth, we either are incapable of recognizing it or take it for false.

We certainly can find our way out of this stage. Yet for this we need to introduce new components into our life that open opportunities[1] for growth. Otherwise it lasts eternally.

When we leave this stage (even if only for brief moments of insights), we proceed directly to the fourth stage (*avirata-samyaktva*) without experiencing *gunasthana* two and three.

2 - **The second *gunasthana* (*sasadana*)** is an interim level we transit while falling from the third to the first stage. In this second stage delusion and error begin to take hold on us. The clear understanding we still could have regained in the third stage is already lost with only a vague memory remaining. The time spent on this level lasts only seconds.

3 - **In the third stage (*misra*)** clear understanding and delusion exist simultaneously in mixed form. We experience this as an ambivalent state. We neither want to separate us from delusion and er-

---

[1] All components necessary for this process already exist within us and in our immediate environment. We only need to recognize them, direct our attention towards them and then activate them for our growth.

'KARMA - THE MECHANISM', chapter 'ATTRACTION TO KARMA', commentary to Sutra 12 describes what conditions enable the spontaneous experience of more advanced stages of development.

ror to regain the clear understanding of the fourth stage, nor do we let go of our clear understanding to move back into the familiar hypnotic environment of level one. As soon as this equilibrium is disturbed and a tendency towards clear understanding or delusion is started, we leave this stage either in the direction of the fourth *gunasthana* (*avirata-samyaktva*) or towards the second (*sasadana*).

The third level can only be reached from the fourth level. Its maximum duration is limited to 48 minutes.

The third stage has enormous significance for our development. Here an important process takes place that stabilizes our access to the clear understanding of the fourth stage.

Many who dwell mainly in the first stage experience flashes of insights into the fourth stage. This is usually a fleeting sensation that feels like a brief, but intense awakening from some long and almost hypnotic 'waking dream'. The sensation is generally regarded as highly agreeable and almost always accompanied by flash-backs to similarly fleeting states we experienced before. Many perceive these brief insights in regular intervals (every 3 to 6 weeks). Most often they occur in times of relative quietness.[2]

Once we understand the nature of these insights, accept them as real and direct our attention towards them, they become livelier and more intense. We remember them more clearly and the ambivalence of the third stage - the simultaneous perception of clear understanding and delusion - occurs.

If at the time this happens we make a *conscious effort* to *regain* the clear understanding of the fourth stage, a momentum is created that eventually, but unfailingly causes the transfer of our

---

[2] Since the West offers no explanation for these perceptions, and since they seem so fleeting, we - after some brief irritation - usually store them in the same place as all the other unexplained experiences which accompany our life and which we choose to ignore as well.

awareness from the first stage to the fourth - irrespective whether each single effort is successful or not.

The fact that we stay only briefly in this stage should not cause disregard for its importance. The third *gunasthana* (*misra*) is a vital instrument for gaining access to higher stages of existence.

4 - In the fourth stage (*avirata-samyaktva*) we reach a clear, intuitive and true understanding of the mechanisms of this world. We are no longer subjected to the strongest form of negative passionate emotions that previously overshadowed us completely, yet our life can still be impeded considerably by the three lesser intense degrees. We make some efforts to gain freedom from karmic limitations, but do not raise sufficient energy for reaching the fifth *gunasthana* (*desavirata*).

In this stage we still are subject to doubt and to the attachment or rejection of material objects. In the first two phases of this stage we can lose our clear understanding (our intuitive orientation towards growth) again. In this case we fall to the third stage (*misra* - mixed truth and delusion), from where we may rise again to the fourth level or - passing through the second level - fall down to the first stage of total delusion.

The fourth *gunasthana* is reached directly from the first stage - without any intermediary steps.

We experience this stage in three phases which differ significantly in their clarity of understanding. The differing character of these phases is caused by the length of time we stay in them.

- The first phase is characterized by fleetingness.

At the first occurrence of this phase all karma (all our emotional attachments to the restrictive mechanisms of level 1) that previously prevented the shift of our awareness to level four becomes inactive (latent) for a short time.

We experience this as brief periods during which all our desires, preoccupations, prejudices and attachments that bonded us to the dense hypnotic envelope of level one cease to engage our attention. It feels as if we all of a sudden wake up from a deep day-dream that the hustle-bustle of daily life constantly weaves around our consciousness.

Yet though we experience this awakening with extraordinary clarity, our desire for the emotional density on level one is so intense that after a brief time (initially after only fractions of seconds, at most after 48 minutes) we fall down to level three, two or one. As long as we do not direct our attention towards these moments of awakening, they continue to be so evanescent that only fleeting impressions remain.

Once we direct attention towards these insights, they lose their fleeting character. In consequence the initial stark contrast to the hypnotic envelope of level one diminishes. We begin to notice that we lose ourselves less and less in the actions we are involved in. The clarity in our life increases and we become able to steer it more consciously. Eventually we exceed the maximum time we can stay in this phase and thereby automatically advance to phase two.

- <u>During the second phase</u> some part of the karma that had only become inactive (latent) in the first phase, dissolves completely. We begin to understand the limiting character of some of our attachments, desires and beliefs that trapped us on level one. We stop refueling these bonds with new energy and attention and in consequence they cease to influence us a short while later. This automatically lengthens the periods during which we are free from the hypnotic envelope that overshadowed our consciousness on level one.

Yet since not all blocking karma has been dissolved, we still lose this state of clarity from time to time. The emotions that then draw us to the lowest level can be so overpowering that we again become fully entangled in the hypnotic cocoon of level 1. In this case we may easily forget the clarity of stage 4 or think it irrelevant and will certainly not attempt to regain the higher state.

When - at the end of this phase - all obstructing karma (i.e. all preocciupations that attached our consciousness to the hypnotic envelope of level one) dissolves, we enter phase three.

- In the third and stable phase of stage four no karmic bonds are able to totally impede the clarity of our understanding any more. To what extent we can put our new insights *into action* depends on the amount of energy we invest in our further growth. To raise sufficient energy for reaching the next *gunasthana* is the basic challenge we face in this third phase.

The transition from phase two to three is so gradual that we become hardly aware of it. Since in phase two we already experienced long stretches of inner clarity, we barely notice that we do not fall back to level one any more. No special experience marks this particular transition other then that the silver lining of awareness of ourselves never disappears again. We might e.g. still feel intense anger, but in contrast to level one now a detached observer in our head always judges our actions and emotions with impartiality, distance and clarity. We now *know* without fail when we do something detrimental to our growth (and still keep on doing it). But we also recognize clearly the activities and attitudes that enhance our growth. The more we listen to this impartial part of us that became aware of itself on this level, and the more we dare to transform our insights into action, the faster higher stages open up.

Though at this point we may feel unsure which activities will further our growth, this insight comes to us the faster the more we desire further progress.

Once we reach this stable phase of stage four, we never fall down to any of the lower *gunasthanas* any more. The far more comprehensive understanding of stage four automatically dissolves all our emotional attachment to the themes (karmas) of stage one to three, which then dissipate *without manifesting much of an effect*.

It is possible to reach this stable phase within one year. It only depends on the sincerity of our interest and the amount of energy we invest in this venture.

Yet this stable phase of stage four has a highly static character. We now can easily get trapped in a complacency that prevents our ascent to higher levels as intensely as the dense emotional cocoon that trapped us on stage one.[3] We now *know* what feelings and activities we need to change, but decline to transfer this insight *into action*. Yet if we do not raise the additional energy required for further progress, our stay in the fourth stage will last eternally.

The rise to the fifth stage (*desavirata*) only becomes possible when a strong and dynamic desire for further development exists *that is also transformed into action*. *ACTIVITY* is the main key that will tilt our life towards the higher stages. Only when we concentrate considerable energy on transferring our insights into decisions and concrete action do we become able to break the karmic stagnation of level four.

---

[3] This often manifests as the conviction that we are progressing well on our path to liberation, - as a smug, self-satisfied contentment with the stability with which we seem to grow, - as a tendency to observe rather than to actively shape our life, - as a preference for techniques or ritual and symbolic action instead of facing the (possibly uncomfortable) challenges necessary for gaining real understanding, - as an adherence to well-know, established paths instead of actively and intelligently confronting inner and outer conflicts, - and as a reluctance to define higher goals for us.

Yet in reality this is stagnancy. What is lacking are the sweeping breakthroughs, the dynamic unfoldment of higher stages, the pronounced transition into far superior levels of our being. Though we might well gain insights in this static phase, we basically are unwilling to raise the energy necessary for any breakthrough to higher stages.

Any attempt to orient our life along the Five Freedoms[4] helps to set further development in motion. Yet in contrast to a widespread interpretation taking a _purely formal_ vow to practice the Five Freedoms is _not_ sufficient to cause the transfer of our awareness to level five.

5 - **The rise to the fifth stage (_desavirata_)** accelerates our progress towards freedom from all karmic limitations significantly in comparison to any of the preceding stages. While on the fourth level we reached clear _mental_ insight into the functioning of the world, on this fifth level we use this clarity to _consciously direct our action_ towards the ultimate freedom. We are carried by an energy previously unknown that amplifies all our efforts.[5] We feel the profound inner urge to explore more advanced levels of understanding and recognize with increasing clarity which of the many possible lines of action in our daily life point towards real freedom.

On this level we recognize the Five Freedoms as the main lines of action that lead in this direction. Although we succeed only partially and imperfectly to put them into practice, we fully comprehend the potential and scope the Freedoms open up for us: We experience more intense levels of compassion and an increasing grasp on truth. We become aware how our entire environment supports our path. We sense the unfoldment of inner growth. The more we detach our emotions from material objects and worries, the more we experience a freedom never tasted before.

The fifth _gunasthana_ is mainly characterized by the following theme: Though we fully recognize the potential the Five Free-

---

4 see 'FIVE FREEDOMS'

5 We get a notion of this mechanism when we work on projects that inspire us intensely. Though the work might be mentally and physically exhausting, our inspiration fuels us far beyond our usual limits of energy and ability.

doms offer us, we _consciously reject_ to transfer all this insight into action. We _know_ exactly what activities and emotions we need to change, _but don't act_ accordingly.

This is caused by the manifestation of a particular type of karma (_pratyakhyanavarana kashaya_) that is the main issue of the fifth level. The more we realize that _only we_ shape our development and the better we transfer this insight into action, the faster we will recognize more fascinating dimensions of our life. The more we understand that our progress depends _exclusively_ on how much energy we invest into the realization of the Five Freedoms, the more our thrust in this direction is amplified by our surroundings.

The transfer from stage 4 to stage 5 can be compared to the beginning of a new 'Jogging'-program. Initially we _know_ that we need to do something for our body. Yet though we _intend_ to start the program, we always put it off until the 'next' day. Finally we really start jogging, but for some days experience only the effort without really enjoying it. We need to raise considerable energy to carry through with it. - Up to this point our experience corresponds to the characteristics of stage 4, - we do something, but are not successful enough to gain more energy than we invest in it.

Then - after 10 to 12 days - we notice changes within us. We are more energetic, more dynamic and feel a distinctly different bodily presence. Our jogging runs more automatic now and we begin to enjoy it. - In a similar way we experience the transition from stage 4 to stage 5. Our new course of action that felt unfamiliar and strenuous initially, now yields first positive results. We feel encouraged and notice that we now steer our life far more efficiently than ever before.

Temporarily our consciousness can still be overpowered by intense manifestations of karma which for a while may dominate all our actions and moods. Unable to fully control our behavior during these outbreaks, the constant and perfect pursuit of the Five Freedoms is not yet possible.

6 - **The sixth level** (*pramatta virata*) is our long desired breakthrough into tangible superior understanding. At the first unfolding of this stage we feel immersed in an intense vividness of the present never before experienced. Immense relief sweeps through our consciousness, dissolving all our worries and fears. We reach unknown heights of serenity, sovereignty and elation. It is as if an inner light has been switched on. - This breakthrough gives us the ultimate and solid confirmation that our path really leads to dimensions of consciousness entirely unimaginable on lower stages.

With liberating clarity we recognize how severely the thought- and emotional patterns of our past and the expectations (and dreads) we project onto the future limit our perception of the present. The immediacy with which we recognize these deep-rooted patterns enables us to consciously break free from their overshadowing influence.

One by one all concepts, emotions, preconceptions and prejudices that up to this moment locked our consciousness into narrow limits, fall off like superfluous crusts. The tight band of events we previously felt and thought was our only conceivable path, now appears like a confining tube in which our life ran from a restrictive past into an equally restricted future.[6] Our awareness begins to perceive the world *outside* this tube.

---

[6] It is easy to demonstrate how past emotions and their projection onto our future restrict the intensity of our present. - We all know the anxiety in the waiting room of a dentist when we expect a highly uncomfortable treatment. We anticipate the pain the doctor might possibly inflict, all our previous painful experiences in a dentist's chair frighteningly vivid before our mind.

This exclusive selective memory of painful moments of the past influences our anticipation of what the next hour might bring us so intensely that we hardly perceive the present. Distractedly we leaf through a magazine. Yet though our eyes are reading the words, we

We recognize that *the sum total of actions possible within the context of the material world is limited*. We now see the entirety of our material world from an outside perspective. For the first time we become aware that our real personality is far greater than the small part we perceive of it within the frame of our incarnations.

We now are free to choose entirely new lines of thoughts and actions independent of any previous mental and emotional patterns. A feeling of universal love rises within us that is not constrained by personal expectations and demands any more. In the beginning we feel like intoxicated by the potential that now opens up for our life.

Our attention shifts from the *fleeting* aspect of the present to its *comprehensive* character. More and more we now become aware of all the associations, expectations, contents and concepts that subconsciously *also* resonate within us when we observe events.

We sense significances and meanings that exist *beyond our senses*.

In each event we confront, we recognize how much we can learn from it if we engage in it through our action, - and how much energy we need to invest to gain these insights.

Yet our experience of this superior understanding is not stable. We drift in and out of this state. One moment we are deeply immersed and shaken by the worries and fears that challenge us

---

barely understand them, our present so totally overshadowed by dire memories and dread of the future.

And then we sit in the chair. The dentist examines us briefly and states that he would not operate on us today. - All our expectations and dreads amounted to nothing. All our projections of the future needlessly obscured our very present.

In the sixth stage of development we dissolve most of this restriction of the present that previously seemed inescapable. - And the relief we feel when we get out of the chair is only a small foretaste of the excitement we will experience, when we free *all* our present from the restrictive memories of our past and the narrow expectations and dreads we habitually project onto our future.

on lower levels, - and in the next our awareness propels us high above these narrow bounds and enables us to imperviously observe them from a distant and uninvolved perspective.

The key to *stabilizing* the sixth stage of development is our decision to expand beyond our emotional attachment to limiting themes of life. The initial euphoric feeling when we entered this level marks the spot (the emotion) where to direct our attention to further disentangle our consciousness from the confining material experiences it is surrounded by.

If we experience *just once* how the sixth stage feels like - even if only for a short time - we become able to reach it *deliberately*. Whenever we confront limiting emotional attachments to the lower levels, we now can consciously decide whether to keep on experiencing the familiar, cherished painful feelings or to rise to stage six.

This is not renunciation, but rather *the conscious decision to remain on a higher level of understanding*. We do not give up our material conditions. We do not try to remove the factors that 'produced' our attachment to lower levels, we only extract our awareness from these confining bounds. We simply choose to orient towards far more attractive, sovereign and serene dimensions within us. We let go of our emotional attachment to some parts of the material world because we recognize how much they constrain our consciousness.

The restricting conditions might well continue to exist, - but only on a lower level that now hardly holds our attention. Since we invest no further energy in them, they completely cease to engage our attention after some time.[7]

---

7 One example: Most of us probably know the hurt we feel when a person we are in love with does not return our affections. When this hurt is triggered, it often overshadows all our emotions and severely distracts our mind. Once we rise to the sixth level, we see this hurt as a minor cloud that overshadows only a small area of our consciousness - which we now perceive as far larger than on level five.

Any activity we recognize as necessary, we now perform far more efficiently since we don't allow our energy to be diverted from our objective by petty egoistic motivation any more.

We realize that _all_ our action furthers our progress.

The greater the courage with which we let go of deepest egoistic motivations, the faster our consciousness expands.

We recognize that we waste valuable energy when we allow our attention to be distracted by irrelevant themes - often manifesting in form of pointless gossip or as the 'endless running commentary' with which our mind incessantly accompanies the banalities of daily life. We observe how this detains other people (and us) on lower levels.[8] We perceive how the contents of such chatter surround us like a cocoon that obstructs any further unfoldment of our consciousness. We consciously extract ourselves from this cocoon.

The 'incessant running commentary' ceases automatically once we begin to systematically direct our attention towards inner growth mechanisms each time we become aware that we engage in this type of pointless (inner) chatter.

Though we still experience karmic manifestations that prevent the perfect realization of the Five Freedoms, these manifestations now surface as mere temporary distractions.

The more our experience of level six stabilizes, the more trying become the emotional challenges we face, when unfulfilled de-

---

[8] This means small talk about money, women, men, food, politics, crimes, accidents, enmities, art, the stupidity and defects of others, sex, scandal, rumors, half-truths etc.

Small talk definitely has its purpose. As long as we are unable to _directly_ fine-tune our relationship with others (which is necessary for the coexistence of human beings), small talk often represents the outer occasion, while the real emotional communication happens on deeper levels (we use this mechanism on level 1 to 5).

Yet during a major unfolding of our consciousness talk about these themes significantly disturbs our process of expansion.

sires prompt us to go back to the violent emotional density of lower levels. It seems as if ever deeper levels of attachment to sore emotions activate so we might go through them for a last time to get rid of them for good. When these temporary distractions occur, patience and perseverance always help to gain back level six.

As soon as we gain sufficient stability to experience the intensity of the present (phase 1) permanently, and we let go enough of our emotional attachment to limiting mechanisms of our material environment to perceive beyond the five outward senses, we enter phase 2. Here we oscillate between stage six and seven until we become familiar enough with the far higher energies and perceptions of stage seven to proceed further.

7 - **From the seventh level (*apramatta virata*)** onwards karmic manifestations (limiting themes of life) cease to overshadow our consciousness. Though we still experience them, we are so thoroughly established in the perception of our greater potential that they are unable to unbalance us.

More and more clearly we now perceive the mechanisms by which our consciousness forms our environment. We see how our emotions, desires and our attachments to ideas, concepts etc. act like magnets that attract the conditions in which these longings can be physically expressed. We begin to use this insight creatively to structure perfect circumstances for our growth. In a most natural and automatic way this environment is in complete harmony with the Five Freedoms. All our being now orients towards unfolding the fantastic potential of our consciousness we sense within.

We reach the seventh level as soon as the perception of our serene and distant self becomes more constant. We accelerate this process when we consciously decide to maintain our superior, peaceful perception of the seventh state instead of succumbing to the limiting emotional attachments that characterize the lower levels.

We experience the seventh stage of development in two phases:

- The first phase of the seventh level is basically a transition-period during which we stabilize the perception of our serene and sovereign self that began to unfold in the sixth stage. Yet on our current level the stability of this perception has a far more assured, profound, superior character than on the sixth level.

  This first phase is characterized by rapid oscillations between level six and seven until we get used to the far more intense energies of the higher stage. For a maximum of 48 minutes we remain in level seven and then fall back to level six. But here we also only stay for a short time before we ascend again.

  We experience this as a constant alternation between rising excitement for the new dimensions we sense opening and doubt and worry that hold us back. The excitement draws us up, while doubt and worry (i.e. manifestations of our lingering fondness for the familiar themes of lower levels) hold us back.

  Fear and worry what an expansion of consciousness might do to us and how our social environment would react is only a residue of past attachments that soon dissolves completely. The path to freedom from all karmic restrictions is never characterized by mounting anxieties, but only by the _dissolution_ of all our fears and also by ever growing assuredness, confidence and insight.

  While in this phase, we are unable to experience any of the higher _gunasthanas_.

- Once we enter the second phase of level seven, we are caught by a sweeping current that pulls our consciousness up into ever more comprehensive stages of development. Where before we needed effort to reach the higher levels, we now are carried by a surge of boundless energy.

The transition between the first and second phase takes us through several stages:

- First we reduce the intensity of the four main negative emotions - anger, pride, dishonesty, greed - by realizing that they really affect _only limited_ areas of our life. We recognize e.g. that anger we feel towards a particular person or situation does not need to influence our _entire_ feeling of life. We compartmentalize this anger, look at it dispassionately and then dissolve it by consciously raising above it.

- In the second stage we experience an extraordinary acceleration of our thoughts. Thousands upon thousands of thinking hours become compressed to mere seconds, to mere flashes of mental images. Our thinking and intuition merge into one. Towering consequences build on each other in our awareness, but with a precise grasp on reality as clear as never before.

  Within (a maximum of 48) minutes we reach dimensions of consciousness entirely unimaginable on lower levels. Yet the higher we go, the more natural and comfortable we handle the fantastic features of our consciousness that now unfold.

- As we rapidly comprehend more and more of reality, we recognize the real origin (_adhikarana_) of any restricting circumstances and the cause of our tendency to choose limiting actions and instantly remove our bonds to them. We dissolve all attachments that impede our upward path, leaving parts of reality that kept us confined before.

We reach this second phase as soon as we relinquish our attachment to the four main negative emotions and cherished, but obstructing action-mechanisms of the lower levels.

After we went through these preparatory stages, the second phase of level seven offers us two paths for further progress:

1 - _The suspension of karma_ - On this path most our remaining karma recedes into a latent, inactive state. Since up to _gunasthana_ eleven inactive karma does not obstruct progress, we become able to experience the character of the higher stages. The path leads via level 8, 9 and 10 to level 11.

Yet we are unable to maintain this stage and have to go back to lower levels. The ascent beyond level 11 is blocked as long as the existing latent karma (i.e. our inactive emotional attachments to experiences on lower levels) obstructs further advancement.

It is not required to _experience_ level 7 to 11 sequentially. We may e.g. bypass all these levels to get a feeling for _gunasthana_ 11 and then later go back at will to explore any of the levels we sidestepped.

2 - _The dissolution of karma_ - On this path we dissolve our remaining karma once and for all. It bypasses level 11 and leads via level 8, 9, 10, 12 and 13 to level 14 and then to ultimate freedom. Though initially this may take us only up to level 11 until _all_ our residual karmic attachments to levels 8 to 11 are dissolved, this path is the sure way to freedom from all karmic limitation.

In the seventh and higher stages pleasure and pain - as we knew them on the lower levels - still manifest as the respective karmas mature. Yet these feelings now hardly attract our attention. We presently are far more in touch with our own eternal character that was merely suppressed by our attachment to karma. With intense joy we feel radiant bliss nearby that attracts us far more than any pleasure or pain the lower stages might offer.

As we follow the path of 'suspension of karma' that takes us rapidly from level 7 to level 11 and down again, we may at will stop at any of the *gunasthanas* we want to experience more closely. An analogy would equal this to a circular subway-system that gives us the option to get in or out at any particular station.

From the seventh level onwards we are far more in control of our fate than ever before. We may at any time choose to dissolve our final emotional attachments to karmic limitations and to proceed to level 12 and finally to ultimate freedom.

But we also have the choice of temporarily going back to stage four or five (though never to stage 1, 2 or 3), if we feel that the experience of particular events or emotions in these stages may enrich our scope of life and be necessary for our further progress. During our return to these (emotionally far denser) levels we may lose much of our previous higher insights until only a vague memory remains. Yet our time on the lower levels is limited. After completing the desired experience, we automatically raise again to the higher level we came from.

8 - **On the eighth level (*apurva karana*)** entirely new and unknown abilities open up. Our consciousness recognizes itself in everything it encounters. Though mild forms of passions still arise, we experience immense delight in either dissolving them or checking their consequences. From this stage onwards the practice of the highest form of meditation (*shukla dhyana* - 'white mediation') becomes possible. *shukla dhyana* is the instrument that enables us to achieve ultimate freedom.

9 - **In the ninth *gunasthana* (*anivritta karana*)** we experience an expansion of the abilities of the eighth level.

10 - **In the tenth stage (*suksma samparaya*)** we dissolve or deactivate even the subtlest forms of greed.

11 - **On stage eleven (*upa shanta moha*)** we begin to perceive the real splendor and majesty of our consciousness for the first time. We get a notion of the eternal, majestic being we really are beyond the limits of this universe.

We now experience our existence within the limited material frame of the body as only a small part of our being, - like a puppet-master who directs his figurines through an animated performance, but commands for himself an immeasurably greater, cosmic understanding that extends far beyond all meaning of the enacted play.

Our eyes look upon the activities of the corporeal part of our self with boundless loving understanding and in infinite peace and certainty that _all_ paths our embodied self may choose will bring it to the desired goal, - irrespective of how much our 'small' self in bodily form understands this process, or how troubled it is by the events it confronts.

This subtle insight into the real nature of our existence becomes possible, because all our deluding karma is inactive (latent) in this stage. As we temporarily extricate our consciousness from all limiting influence, we get a first glimpse what freedom from all karma will be like. This temporary insight into our real, magnificent character enables us to _consciously_ decide when to dissolve our last emotional attachment to limiting karmas. We now do not blindly enter an unknown, mysterious state, but know exactly where we go, when we irrevocably choose our path to ultimate freedom.

At the end of our stay on level eleven the latent deluding karmas become active again, our longing for further experiences within material limits again takes over our consciousness and we go back to level seven, eight, nine or ten. From there we may ascend again.

Once we choose the path of complete dissolution of our karmas (see *gunasthana* 7), we proceed directly from level ten to level twelve.

12 - **The twelfth stage (*kshina moha*)** can only be reached from stage ten. In stage twelve we dissolve all karmas that produce delusion. In consequence this causes the shedding of the last karmas that still blocked knowledge and intuition and caused obstructions. Shortly before reaching stage thirteen, sleep and deep sleep end. Our consciousness reaches clarity unknown. We now cease to be at the mercy of karmic forces, but are the perfect master of our life. Our ultimate freedom is ensured.

13 - **In the thirteenth *gunasthana* (*sayoga kevali*)** we reach the state of omniscience (*kevali*). Our consciousness now encompasses the totality of knowledge. If we have bound special *tirthankara-karma*, we teach on this level. Activity - *yoga* - is the only influence we are still subjected to. And this last bond we dissolve at our ascent to level fourteen.

14 - **The fourteenth *gunasthana* (*ayoga kevali*)** immediately precedes ultimate freedom. Here we separate our consciousness from our last remaining karmic bonds. We liberate ourselves from status, emotions, body and limiting time and thereby dissolve all restrictive connections to the non-living elements (*ajiva dravyas*). We leave the fetters of the entire strata of bodily existence to regain full command of our greater, majestic self, - immensely enriched by our experiences in the restricted, separated circumstances we voluntarily and consciously subjected ourselves to.

The moment we reach ultimate freedom we again assume what was never really lost to us, - pure unrestricted consciousness. We now fully experience our inherent nature - unlimited cognition, unlimited love, unlimited knowledge, unlimited power and timeless bliss.

Each higher stage brings about a substantial acceleration of development and our ability to comprehend. This acceleration can be compared to the mechanism of an e-curve, which after a long, drawn-out starting-phase with only few small changes, rapidly increases in dynamic to reach the final state only a short time later.

Though we may spend long time in *gunasthana* one and four, we should not infer that the higher stages require an equal amount of time for their unfoldment. From the fifth *gunasthana* onwards we experience an unprecedented acceleration of our development that cannot even be imagined in the preceding stages.

This acceleration is further supported by the fact that entire groups of karmas that are active only on a lower stage, automatically fall off once we stabilize our consciousness on a higher level. The broader and more comprehensive understanding of the new level automatically dissolves our emotional attachment to these themes of life (karmas), which then dissipate *without manifesting much of an effect*.

Though this may sound like magic, it is nothing other than what we experience while growing up. Tasks that needed all our energy and attention when we were in the playing pen - e.g. putting three wooden blocks on top of each other - cease to occupy our attention as soon as we grow out of them. Though we could build far better towers when we are 16, we would never even think of doing so.

We can use this mechanism to accelerate our development significantly. If - instead of 'battling' annoying and limiting theses of life on the level on which they occur - we shift our attention to higher levels, these themes will dissipate in a similar way as they did in the playing pen.

This description is a brief overview. The characteristics, mechanisms and inner logic of the *gunasthanas* are far more extensive and complex than can be covered in this book. For deeper understanding it is recommended to read *Gommatasara - Jiva* and *Karma Kanda*.

One word regarding the classification of our own presently active stage of development:

It is safe to assume that almost everyone who reads these lines for the first time spends most of his time in the first level (*mithyaktva*). Yet an interest in the theme of this book indicates that our mind is already searching for opportunities to leave this stage of perpetual delusion.

A realistic evaluation of our own position - without self-deception - is one of the few essentials of a successful journey to far more fascinating levels of existence.

The following diagram shows a visual representation of all 14 stages of development (*gunasthanas*).

The diagram is partitioned into four blocks. Each block comprises several stages that are connected by mechanism of expansion unique to this phase. The subsequent pages explain these blocks in detail.

F R E E D O M

14 *ayoga kevali* - last stage before ultimate freedom
separating our consc. from all limiting influences
limited duration (brief)

13 *sayoga kevali*
omniscience / state of a *tirthankara*
limited duration -

12 *kshina moha*
dissolving all karmas that produce delusion
limited duration

11 *upa shanta moha* - suspended delusion
first glimpse of the real majesty of our consciousness
limited duration

10 *suksma samparaya*
suspending or dissolving all subtle forms of greed
limited duration

9 *anivritta karana*
expanding the new abilities of stage 8
limited duration

8 *apurva karana* - new and unknown abilities
recognizing ourselves in everything we encounter
limited duration

7 *apramatta virata*
karma ceases to overshadow our consciousness

6 *pramatta virata* - vividness of the present
freedom from emotional and thought patterns
Phase 1
limited duration

5 *desavirata* - directing **action** towards freedom
partial transfer of our mental insights into activity
limited duration

4 *samyaktvi* - directing **thoughts** towards freedom
clear **mental** insight how reality functions
Phase 1
max. 48 min.

3 *misra* - learning how to decide for growth
clear mental insight mixed with delusion and error
s
u
d
max. 48 min.

2 *sasadana* - transitory downfall stage
clear mental insight becomes only a vague memory
d
e
1 sec.

1 *mithyaktva* - state of delusion, error, misconceptions
deeply absorbed by emotions, events, activites
n
duration unlimited !

# of our consciousness from all karmic restrictions

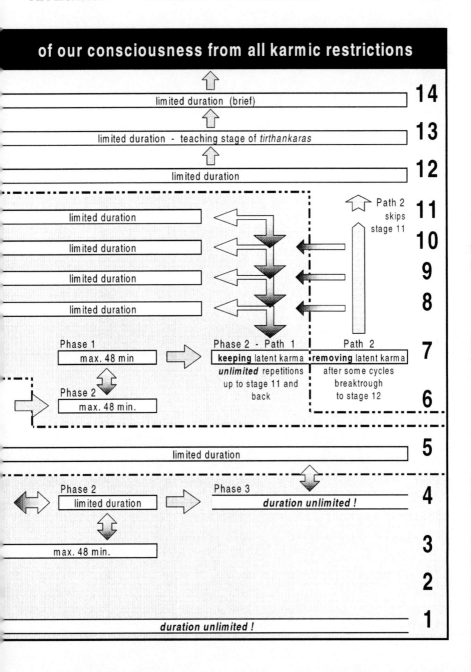

limited duration (brief)   **14**

limited duration - teaching stage of *tirthankaras*   **13**

limited duration   **12**

Path 2 skips stage 11   **11**

limited duration   **10**

limited duration   **9**

limited duration   **8**

limited duration

Phase 1   Phase 2 - Path 1   Path 2   **7**
max. 48 min   **keeping** latent karma   **removing** latent karma
unlimited repetitions   after some cycles
up to stage 11 and   breaktrough
Phase 2   back   to stage 12   **6**
max. 48 min.

limited duration   **5**

Phase 2   Phase 3   **4**
limited duration   *duration unlimited !*

max. 48 min.   **3**

2

duration unlimited !   **1**

PART 1 - Stage 1 - 4

Leaving the dense emotional envelope our everyday activities weave around our consciousness.

Discovering our ability to shift our attention to more advanced stages.

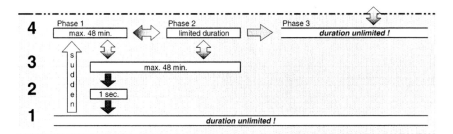

In stage 1 we are still deeply caught up in all our emotions, activities and events. Yet almost everyone experiences unexpected, brief insights into stage 4.

This feels as if we all of a sudden wake up from a day-dream-like state. Though initially these insight are very brief, we experience them with great clarity and often remember similar incidences in our past. Encounters of this kind usually occur every 3 - 6 weeks. They are highly agreeable.

For the duration of this insight, we perceive stage 4. Our attention shifts directly from stage 1 to stage 4 without perceiving level 2 and 3.

We experience stage 4 in three phases.

In the first phase our insights remain fleeting. As long as we do not direct our attention there, we never experience more than brief impressions. In this case we fall back to the level of delusion (stage 1) after only minutes or seconds while passing stage 3 or 2.

Yet once we direct our attention towards these insights, they automatically lose their fleeting character so we become able to perceive them longer and clearer. We then also have a clearer perception of stage 3 where our clear understanding of level 4 and the delusion and prejudices of level 1 exist *simultaneously and parallel* to each other. Here we can decide whether to give in to the attraction of the familiar hypnotic envelope of level 1 and fall down to it, or to raise the energy to again reach the clarity of level 4.

It is the purpose of stage 3 to train us in this decision. Though initially not every effort to re-establish the clarity of level 4 might be successful, we create a momentum that eventually but unfailingly will permanently transfer our awareness from stage 1 to stage 4.

After some time we exceed the maximum time we can stay in this phase and thereby automatically advance to phase two. Yet even in phase 2 we lose this state of clarity from time to time and fall back to delusion and prejudices. Depending on the strength of the emotions that draw us to this lowest level, we can become so involved in its hypnotic envelope that we completely forget the clarity of stage 4 or regard it for so unimportant that we invest no effort into regaining it.

Yet when we take every slipping into the envelope of stage 1 as an incentive to increase our efforts to again reach level 4, we stabilize our awareness of the higher stage. We then proceed from its second phase to the third phase, from where we do not fall down to stage 1 any more. This transition is not marked by a clear experience like our sudden ascent from stage 1 to stage 4. We only notice that the silver lining of our conscious perception of the awareness of our self never disappears again.

The permanent shift of our awareness from stage 1 to stage 4 can be reached within one year. This only depends on how seriously we are interested in progressing and how much energy we invest in this undertaking.

PART 2 - Stage 5 - 6

Consciously choosing and accomplishing selected activities to free ourselves from limiting material events.

Gaining the skill to leave restrictive emotions behind.

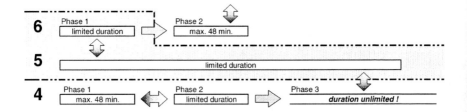

In the stable phase (3) of stage 4 we reached clear understanding of the real functioning of the world. To proceed to stage 5, we need to transfer this *mental* insight into *action*.

Yet the stable phase (3) of stage 4 is highly static. We here get easily trapped in a complacency that prevents our ascent to higher levels as intensely as the dense emotional cocoon that trapped us on stage one. We might well experience some seeming growth of understanding, if we do not raise the energy to break out of this static contentment, our stay in stage 4 will last eternally.

ACTIVITY is the main key that tilts our life towards the higher stages.

Stage 5 is mainly characterized by the following theme: Though we fully recognize the potential the Five Freedoms offer us, we *consciously reject* to transfer all this insight into action. We *know* exactly what activities and emotions we need to change, *but don't act* accordingly. The more we realize that *only we* shape our development and the better we transfer this insight into action, the faster we will recognize more fascinating dimensions of our life. The more we understand that *only we ourselves* are responsibly for our progress, that it is *only we ourselves* who structure our development, and the more we succeed to really transfer this insight into action, the more new and more fascinating dimensions will open up in our life.

Stage 6 is our long desired breakthrough into tangible superior understanding. At the first unfolding of this stage, we feel an intense vividness of the present never before experienced.

With liberating clarity we recognize how severely the thought- and emotional patterns of our past and the expectations (and dreads) we project onto the future limit our perception of the present. The immediacy with which we recognize these deep-rooted patterns enables us to fundamentally break free from their overshadowing influence.

Yet the first phase of stage 6 is not stable. We drift in and out of this state. The key to stabilizing the sixth stage of development is our *decision* to extricate us from our emotional attachment to limiting themes of life. If we experience *once* how the sixth stage feels like - even if only for a short time - we become able to reach it *deliberately*.

As soon as we gained sufficient stability to experience the intensity of the present - phase 1 - on a more permanent basis, and let go enough of our emotional attachment to limiting mechanisms of our material environment to perceive the world beyond the five outward senses, we enter phase 2.

In phase 2 we oscillate rapidly for some time between stage six and seven until we become comfortable enough with the far higher energies and perceptions of stage seven to proceed further.

PART 3 - Stage 7 - 11

Discovering and exploring the world beyond our senses.
Glimpsing the real majesty of our consciousness and orienting towards experiencing more of it.

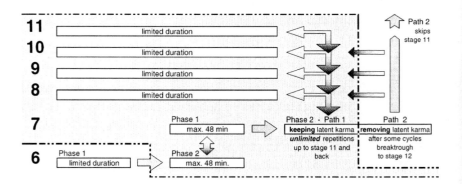

<u>Stage 7</u> we experience in two phases that differ significantly from each other. Phase one is a transition-period during which we become familiar with the more intense energies and abilities that characterize this stage. For some time we oscillate between stage 6 and 7 until we stabilized the perception of our sovereign higher self that began to unfold from stage 6 onwards.

In phase two we are caught by a sweeping current that pulls our consciousness up into ever more comprehensive stages of development. The transition between the first and second phase takes us through several stages, during which our mental processes accelerate so intensely that an entirely new comprehension of reality opens up within us.

After we went through these preparatory stages, the second phase of level seven offers us two paths for further progress:

1 - *The suspension of karma* - On this path most our remaining karma recedes into a latent, inactive state. Since latent karma does not obstruct our progress up to stage 11, we become able to experience the character of the higher stages. Yet we are unable to maintain this high state and always fall back to the lower stages. The ascent beyond level 11 is blocked as long as our temporary inactive, yet nevertheless existing emotional attachments to experiences on lower levels (i.e. our undissolved latent karma) obstructs all further advancement.

It is not required to *experience* level 7 to 11 sequentially. We may e.g. bypass all these levels to get a feeling for stage 11 and then later go back at will to explore any of the levels we sidestepped.

Stage 8 opens up entirely new and hitherto unknown abilities. We recognize ourselves in everything we encounter.

In stage 9 we experience an expansion of the abilities of stage 8.

In stage 10 we dissolve or deactivate even the subtlest forms of greed.

In stage 11 we begin to perceive the real majesty and splendor of our consciousness for the first time. We get a notion of the eternal, majestic being we really are beyond the limits of this universe.

At the end of our stay in stage 11 the latent deluding karmas become active again, our longing for further experiences within material limits again takes over our consciousness and we go back to level seven, eight, nine or ten. From there we may ascend again.

2 - *The dissolution of karma* - On this path we dissolve our remaining karma once and for all.

PART 4 - Stage 7 - 14 and beyond

Consciously deciding to experience the majesty of our consciousness without restrictions.

Reaching all-comprehensive understanding and ultimate freedom from all limiting circumstances.

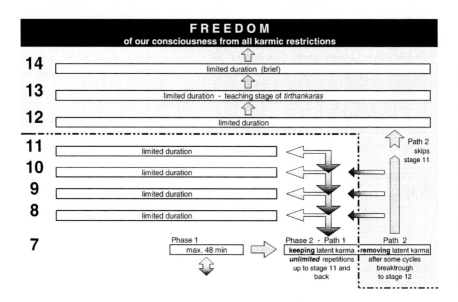

When we choose the _dissolution of all karma_ in the second phase of stage 7, we fundamentally decide for reaching ultimate freedom.

This path bypasses level 11 and leads via level 8, 9, 10, 12 and 13 to level 14 and then to ultimate freedom. Though initially this may take us only up to level 11 until _all_ our karmic attachments to levels 8 to 11 are dissolved, this path is the sure way to freedom from all karmic limitation.

Stage 12 can only be reached from level ten. On level twelve we dissolve all karmas that produce delusion. In consequence this causes the shedding of the last karmas that still blocked knowledge and intuition and caused obstructions. We now are no more at the mercy of karmic forces, but the perfect master of our life. We will reach the ultimate freedom for sure.

In stage 13 we reach omniscience (*kevali*). Our consciousness now encompasses the totality of knowledge.

If we have bound *tirthankara*-karma, we transfer our know-how from this level. Activity - *yoga* - is the only influence we are still subjected to. And this last bond we dissolve at our ascent to level fourteen.

Stage 14 immediately precedes ultimate freedom. Here we separate us from our last desires for limiting experiences (from all our remaining karmic bonds). Free from all fetters of the bodily level we regain full command of our great, majestic self, - immensely enriched by our experiences in the restricted, separated circumstances we voluntarily and consciously subjected ourselves to.

The moment we reach ultimate freedom we again assume what was never really lost to us, - pure unrestricted consciousness. As an enlightened being (*siddha*) we now fully experience our inherent nature - unlimited cognition, unlimited love, unlimited knowledge, unlimited power, and timeless bliss.

FIVE FREEDOMS

The 'Five Freedoms' are five specific lines of action. After reaching the fifth stage of development, we recognize them as the five major types of activities that lead to freedom from all karmic limitations. The Five Freedoms are:

1 - <u>Profound understanding of all living beings and the feeling of natural compassion towards them</u>

We recognize our own aspirations and path in other beings. - This produces a growing awareness how our actions affect others. It leads to a way of life where we automatically take care that our actions do not restrict the vitality and expression of other beings and naturally avoid injuring or killing them.

2 - <u>An intense craving for truth</u>

From the fifth stage of development onwards truth is perceived as all mechanisms that lead from misconception and confusion towards freedom from all karmic limitations. This automatically produces the insight that communicating misleading information, false or unconfirmed rumors and vague statements is essentially damaging, since it promotes and maintains a state of deception in others. We realize that only by living and communicating truth do we create that refined aura of clarity *around ourselves* which enables us to intuitively select from the many alternatives of daily life the one path that leads to real freedom. This attitude makes us naturally express truth in all our speech and action.

3 - The insight that *all* components needed to reach freedom from karmic limitations already exist within us and in our very own environment

It is the awareness that we only need to identify and understand these components to receive optimal support for our path. - Once we realize this, we experience that everything needed for our own development is always provided in abundance. - This automatically produces the insight that any craving for the possessions of others is irrelevant and pointless.

4 - The intention to grow

This is experienced as a burning desire for ever higher dimensions of our consciousness. It is the main drive of our path to ultimate freedom. From the fifth stage of development onwards our intention to grow amplifies our efforts with an additional energy that becomes stronger the more intensely we pursue this direction.

5 - The recognition that material possessions play no significant role for reaching ultimate freedom

We experience matter more and more as only a *partial* aspect of life, whose influence on our growth-process is continuously diminishing. This does not mean to give up all possessions. We only recognize the decreasing importance of material components for our path and consciously support this development.

From the fifth stage of development onward we perceive more and more clearly that these five broad lines of action systematically unfold superior levels of comprehension and are essential for reaching ultimate freedom. This realization imparts an additional, invigorating energy that incites us *to steer our life consciously* along these five main lines.

The Conventional Interpretation

The above interpretation differs significantly from the way the Jains usually interpret the Five Freedoms. According to their understanding the Five Freedoms are:

1 - To be free from killing or hurting living beings - directly or indirectly.

2 - To be free from falsehood, deception and dishonesty.

3 - To be free from taking what is not given voluntarily.

4 - To be free from the inner compulsion that allows sexual needs to govern our life.

5 - To be free from the attachment to material possessions.

The Jains generally interpret the Five Freedoms as 'vows'. Many of them believe that everyone who formally accepts these vows proceeds directly and automatically from the first to the fifth stage of development (*gunasthana*). However, this general understanding does not correspond with the mechanism of the 14 *gunasthanas* as it is described in the ancient scriptures. It rather indicates that much of the basic comprehension of this dynamic method of development has been lost - irrespective of how widely the erroneous understanding may be believed in.

A mere formal acceptance of these vows can never cause the transfer to a higher stage of comprehension and development. Certainly - taking the five vows can mark an initial point from where growth in this direction may start, but *higher stages of development will only unfold when we remove the karma that blocks our perception of these stages*.

Unfortunately the flawed conventional interpretation often leads to much pointless world-renunciation, self-punishment and intense ascetic behavior.

The Five Freedoms are a method of dynamic growth that has *nothing* to do with sacrifice, self-denial or renunciation of the world. On the contrary - feelings of remorse, self-punishment, mortification etc., (which are often associated with sacrifice and renunciation) not only hamper our path to freedom from karma, but may block it altogether. *Self-denial, remorse etc. only indicate a negative bond to the objects and situations denied and not a fundamental freedom from them.* As hate is just proof of a highly emotional attachment to the hated person - only in a negative way - so also remorse, self-denial etc. only indicates a *negative* bond to the resented objects, it does not produce freedom or detachment from them. As long as any object we want to be free from still plays a role in our life, we are not free from it.

Furthermore - any kind of self-denial or remorse always orients towards *past* experiences. It forever looks back to atone for deeds, emotions or thoughts gone by. It never inspires dynamic impulses towards future progress. But as long as we only strive for a freedom *from* something rather than aspiring a freedom *to do* something, we have not found true freedom yet.

The Five Freedoms are *never* directed towards the *sacrifice* of elements of life, but always towards attaining new, more fascinating and broader dimensions of experience. We are reaching this new state because it attracts us more than the old one. That the old state becomes obsolete in this process and falls away, is a side-effect, not the main aim. One example: When we switch from a radio station with 'boring' music to one with a more interesting program, we would never regard this switch as 'sacrificing the boring music', but rather as a nice change for the better.

When we realize the lines of actions the Five Freedoms point out, we waste no energy on any attempt to abolish old conditions, but instead concentrate on the experience of new and more attractive levels of life. The shedding of old conditions and behavior patterns consequently happens automatically, without any forcing.

In the original Sanskrit the Five Freedoms are also called *sanyama* which translates as 'control' or 'steering'. The *conscious steering of our life along the five lines of action* described in the beginning is the real mechanism that leads towards the experience of higher levels of consciousness.

The Intention to Grow

The fourth freedom is customarily interpreted as 'the restraining of sexual activity'. Yet this restrictive understanding does not agree with the dynamism with which the other four freedoms accelerate the expansion of human experience and development.

The Sanskrit-word '*brahma*' denoting this freedom means 'growth', 'evolution', 'expansion'. It is not in any way connected to sexual sense-experiences.[9]

None of the Jaina scriptures offer an explanation why the restriction of one particular sense-experience would cause inner growth. The few dogmatic statements about this subject do not conform to the precision of Jaina knowledge which usually presents quite exhaustive elucidation.

For all these reasons it is probable that between the time and teaching of Mahavir (557 to 527 BC) and the writing of the Tattvarthasutra 700 or 800 years later, the word *brahma* has changed its meaning - as it happened several times in the history of Sanskrit.

Returning to the original meaning of 'expansion' and 'growth' *freedom from non-growth* (*a-brahma*) certainly means *'the intention to grow'*. - which is far more in step with the dynamic expansion that characterizes *all* Jaina knowledge, than its reduction to sexuality.

It certainly is everyone's own decision to interpret *abrahma* in the conventional way. In our modern world this would be *'freedom from the need to always search for (new) sexual partners'*. However, it is recommended to observe whether practicing this interpretation really brings about a noticeable expansion of consciousness.

Yet - irrespective how this is assessed - our very own *'intention to grow'* doubtlessly constitutes the core-element of *any* path to ultimate freedom.

---

[9] The term '*brahmacharya*' is also used. It translates *'the way of life directed towards growth'* and is not connected to sexuality either. Only habitual usage associates *brahma* and *brahmacharya* with a restriction of sexual experience.

REINCARNATION

Karma is easily associated with reincarnation. Not without reason; - though karmic mechanisms definitely operate in the actual present, they also are placed in the context of successive embodiments. The West often looks upon this model with disdain and without much further consideration relegates it to the domain of oriental fairy tales - usually with a mild ironic smile.

But we easily forget that our precious Western idea of existence is also just a concept. The presumption that life is created from nothing to assume a brief corporal existence, then - at its end - is transferred to another type of body to remain rather eternally in heaven or hell, - this presumption originates in religious beliefs hardly accessible to logic.

Ever since science successfully propagated the idea that only what is physically perceived is permitted to exist, heaven and hell are dismissed. Our life (and our consciousness) was reduced to an accidental play of chemicals that neither exists before the body's birth, nor after its death and therefore could not possibly have any deeper meaning.

Now - _every_ concept - whether originating in the divine, scientifically proven or practically tested - is always only a mental model, a pattern projected onto a set of personal experiences. And these patterns always amplify some parts of the experience while ignoring or reducing the relevance of others.

Unfortunately many of these models exclude entire sections of reality which govern highly important mechanisms of life. It is impossible to discover these missing mechanisms from the _inside_ of a concept with only the help of the concept's tools and logic. And it often is very difficult to even get a notion that something else exists _outside_ the cherished model. As long as we rigidly adhere to one single model, there always is the danger that entire sections of reality are inaccessible to us.

Yet we cannot live without concepts. We need a conscious idea how to successfully handle life. But since no concept is capable of embracing the entire latitude, depth and dynamism of our existence, it doesn't make sense to take the _belief_ in _one_ system as the ground to principally reject the serious examination of others.

Karma and reincarnation are also nothing other than concepts projected onto this world. They are not holy and there certainly are areas in which they are not valid. Yet karma and reincarnation encompass a far broader section of reality than many other (Western) models. They open up experiences and mechanisms other concepts do not believe accessible.

Reincarnation manifests our craving to physically experience all the values, ideas and ideals we carry deep within us. Our present life is a very expression of this craving. _What we encounter now IS reincarnation!_ We ourselves consciously attracted all the circumstances we experience at present. We ourselves created all the challenges, the tension, the impossible situations we confront now so as to bring out the values hidden within us. We did and do create this because we were unable to experience the fulfillment of these aspirations in previous lives.

Not everything we want to experience needs necessarily be regarded as positive in the social context in which we incarnate. It may well set us against norms, break rigid rules, upset ourselves and others, and much more, but nevertheless it is all driven by the same intense desire to manifest those values within us. Some of these values might find success, some might face opposition and become failures and some might die off in the process without even leaving a trace. But this is only _one_ part of the learning process we subject ourselves to. The most important thing in all the actions, attitudes and emotions we create is _that we manifest them in the first place_, - is that we do not keep them bottled inside us, - is that we express what we feel within us in the physical world.

When we leave our present body, we take with us all the abundance of the experiences gained by these attempts, all the sagacity, the maturity, the sovereignty we accumulated within us. We might even choose to carry detailed memories into our next lives, but this is rare. Most of us favor to enter a new life unencumbered by the recollection of past events.

Death is a highly overrated experience. It is nothing other than leaving our physical body to experience different levels of existence. It is nothing other than what we experience while we are dreaming. When entering the dream-state, we take it as a self-understood fact that we do not take our physical body with us. It remains behind in bed while we take on a 'dream'-body that feels as real as our physical body. And this 'dream'-body often enables us to experience action far more flexible, intense and exciting than our present conditions would ever permit. We also never lose our identity while entering dreams, we always take the 'I' with us, - and we always feel completely normal and natural in our dream-identity while doing the most extraordinary things.

Though we all experience leaving our physical body several times during sleep each night, we usually do not connect our dream-experiences to the mechanism of death. Yet death is also nothing more than our consciousness leaving our physical body. Sure, it appears different because we do not return to this particular physical body and its familiar environment. But then - have we ever cared much about the many 'dream-bodies' we left behind when waking up? Once our consciousness has left one particular level of perception, our awareness becomes so captivated by the new body and the new environment we then experience that we entirely forget our previous frame of reference - irrespective if we have the option of returning to it (dream) or not (death).

And as we were able to retain our identity, character and memories while entering the dream-world, we also take all our identity, character, wisdom and everything we are and learnt with us at our time of death.

The apprehension with which the West looks upon death stems from the idea that our present life is _the only one_ we will ever have and that - if we botch it - we never will get another chance.

This is a good illustration how rigid concepts can limit our scope of life. As long as we believe that this is our only life, we tend to get as much physical excitement out of it as possible. Especially in our youth we focus almost exclusively on the joy our body can give us. We casually presume that older bodies would be less capable of doing so and that any non-material enjoyment would be more difficult to reach. We hardly ever recognize or even hold possible that alternative dimensions of life may bring far more intense thrills and ecstasy.

Unfortunately this exclusive focus on material enjoyment often carries over into our more mature part of life. Instead of recognizing the limited range of material enjoyment and progressing to more satisfying dimensions, we frequently attempt to re-enact particular positive experiences of our youth - often with less and less success. At the end of our life we then may look back in frustration and with the unspoken question what this was all about. Yet though we certainly will have another opportunity (another life) to figure this out, this is missing the point.

The far more interesting question is - where do we go from there? What is our intention _after_ we leave our physical body?

All the values and ideas we were unable to express in our current life will leave an unfulfilled longing at our time of death. This longing has the tendency to make us again choose circumstances that offer the potential of fulfilling this craving.

Yet it is an illusion to hope that our next life will bring the desired satisfaction if we do not _actively_ take concrete steps necessary for fulfilling our aspirations _NOW_. Only sitting and waiting for something to happen will _never_ produce the desired results - and _NEVER_ in this case means the endless repetition of our present dissatisfying circumstances.

So why not face the challenges we carry within us _now_? If our next lifetime will confront us with similar circumstances as we currently experience, what makes us hope that we will take up the opportunity _then_, if we fail to take charge of manifesting our ideas now, - in the very present?

The idea that this is our very first incarnation and that any successive life in a bodily context is _re_-incarnation, is naïve and illogical. There has been a long chain of lives before this one and there might be an equally long and monotonous chain ahead of us for as long as we continue to avoid manifesting our inner ideals and values.

Now is our point of power. _Now_ is the only point in time when we are able to do something. If we transfer this power to another - future - _re_-incarnation, we basically surrender the control of our life(s) to a diffuse future that will never arrive.

The fact that the theme of this book triggered your interest is the best indication that materially oriented themes do not engage your full interest any more and that you now are - consciously or subconsciously - searching for other and more rewarding realms.

ANCIENT SCRIPTURES

The Jains divide their scriptures into two main types, - those within the classical Canon and those outside it.[10]

The basis for these subdivisions is the stage of development of those who wrote the scriptures:

1 - the *tirthankaras*, who taught from the state of omniscience,

2 - their immediate disciples (*sruta kevalis*) and

3 - the subsequent teachers and leaders of the groups disseminating this knowledge.

Of the wealth of ancient scriptures listed in earlier manuscripts, many have been lost during the last two millennia. Yet still a considerable number reached our present times intact. Unfortunately only

---

[10] The classical Canon is divided into twelve parts: *Acara, Sutrakrita, Sthana, Samavaya, Vyakhyaprajnapti, Jnatridharmakatha, Upasakadhyayana, Antakriddasa, Anuttaraupadikadasa, Prasnavyakarana, Vipakasutra* and *Dristivada.*

Dristivada has five subparts: *Parikarma, Sutra, Prathamanuyoga, Purvagata* and *Culika.*

Purvagata is divided into 14 parts: *Utpadapurva, Agrayaniya, Viryanupravada, Astinastipravada, Jnanapravada, Satyapravada, Atmapravada, Karmapravada, Pratyakhyananamadheya, Vidyanupravada, Kalyanana-madheya, Pranavaya, Kriyavisala* and *Lokabindusara.*

Outside this canon there exist many works, e.g. *Dasavaikalika, Uttaradhyayana* etc.

few of these works have been translated intelligibly into Western languages yet and even these few are often out of print. A CD is presently in preparation that will contain facsimile copies of the major original manuscripts and their existing translations into English language (available at Crosswind Publishing).

The following list contains a short selection of scriptures that deal mainly with the mechanisms of the expansion of consciousness and have been translated into English language:

- *Tattvarthadhigama Sutra* by Sri Umaswami Acharya,
  Original Sanskrit Text with Introduction, Translation, Notes and Commentary in English by J.L.Jaini, Volume II of The Sacred Books of the Jainas, Arrah, India, 1920.

- *Sarvarthasiddhi* by Sri Pujapada,
  The oldest commentary of the Tattvarthasutra, published under the title *Reality* by S.A.Jain, Vira Sasana Sangha, Calcutta, India, 1960.

- *Dravya Sangraha* of Nemichandra,
  Original Text with Introduction, Translation, Notes etc. by S.C.Goshal, The Sacred Books of the Jainas, Arrah, India, 1917.

- *Gommatasara - Jiva and Karma Kanda* by Sri Nemichandra
  Original Text with Introduction, Translation and Commentary by J.L.Jaini, Volume V and IV of The Sacred Books of the Jainas, Lucknow, India, 1927.

WHAT TO DO

Now that you have read the book, the question might arise: - How may I experience all this myself? - What can I do to unfold all these intriguing dormant states of consciousness within myself?'

Well, - first of all, - regard your path to freedom from karmic limitations not as a grave obligation or as a heavy load on you, but rather as an adventure, - a venture of discovery, - a romantic quest for something new and fascinating, - an exciting journey of exploration. There is no compulsion *not* to enjoy your venture. You are not obliged to behave grave, solemn and glum while reaching for the highest, or to regard it as hard work only. It is nowhere stated that you are forbidden to laugh and play and to have fun while you achieve real freedom.

What to do? - Well, - carry out the directions given in 'HOW TO DISSOLVE KARMA' (see 'CHECKLIST FOR REAL GROWTH' at the end of this book) and follow these seven suggestions, - higher dimensions of your consciousness will then become reality automatically:

1 - Become aware of the many insights you already have

Put your attention on your moments of wakefulness, no matter how short and fleeting they are, - on these moments of clear understanding that give you insight into broader and deeper meanings of this world. Become aware that these sudden breakthroughs give you vital information about the many dimensions of consciousness hidden within you.

Remember the emotions that accompany these insights, these breakthroughs and try to re-experience what you felt while they occurred.

As a result your understanding will expand. Your fleeting insights will stabilize and become a natural feature of your life.

2 - Always go for the highest choice

If you can choose between a comfortable and an uncomfortable path, - choose the uncomfortable one, that's the right one for you.

See, you already know the comfortable path, because otherwise how could you possibly recognize that it is more comfortable. What we already know always feels more comfortable. It is _the unknown_ that makes us feel awkward and uneasy. It is always the unknown that requires considerable more energy to face than the familiar.

Choose the uncomfortable path because it will lead you out of the known circle of your life, - it is the one that will break your boundaries, - it is the one that will expand the envelope in which you move.

3 - Really _carry out_ what you intend to do

Initiate the actions you want to experience. Intentionally put yourself into those situations and positions that make you really meet the challenges you want to face.

Try out the path you see in front of you. Do change all the components of your current life you feel need changing.

But don't procrastinate, don't lose yourself in endless preparation. Go ahead through learning by doing.

And don't seek too much advise. Advise from well-meaning friends and relatives is one of the major reasons why well-intentioned projects fail. Especially the people close to you more often than not have not the slightest clue what you are reaching for.

<u>You</u> are shaping your very own, individual path according to your very own needs, - if you are serious about it, you definitely will know what to do, - you don't need much advise.

And if you don't know what to do? - If nothing comes to your mind how to create your path to higher stages, then

4 - Make a list

Make a list of all the things you'd like to do or to become this life. Write down all your aspirations, ideals, dreams, fantasies, everything that comes to your mind, even if it looks utterly absurd to you and even if it does not seem to lead into a spiritual direction:

Do write down the things you want to learn, to master, to apply.

Write down the situations you want to experience, the places to visit, the people you want to meet, to interact and to have fun with.

Write down the honors you want to receive, the amount of money you would like to have and what you will do with it once you attained it.

Write down the challenges you want to meet and how much excitement they should bring to your life.

Write down the adventures you want to experience, and how much risk you are prepared to face on these ventures without known outcome.

Never censure your thoughts while you are writing, - never evaluate whether your desires are feasible or not, whether they appear comfortable or not, whether you are afraid of them or not. Do not even put them in any sequence - like what to do first, what takes priority, what is most or least feasible. All this comes later. During this first step just define that colorful part of yourself you have not manifested yet.

And never regard this list closed. This is only your _very first_ list, add more items any time you like.

Arrange this list according to your preferences.

Then do whatever is necessary to _playfully realize_ all your ideas, desires, fantasies and aspirations. -

Become all what you really want to be.

It will give you self-assuredness, charisma and power.
It will make you aware of new areas of life.
It will alert you to the ways you manifest your dreams.
It will unfold more advanced perception within you.
It will intensify your life.

This process frees you from your dormant desires. Enjoy it! - And at one certain point in time you will notice that you _have become_ what you ever wanted to be and to experience. Now your emotions and mind are free to explore higher levels. Now you perceive the higher avenues that previously were clouded by dormant desires you did release through action.

There is no need to hasten this process, but keep at it steadily.

5 - _LIVE_ instead of only watching TV

If you want your life to be interesting, stop watching TV. TV takes all your creativity, energy and focus and dumps it into the low-level reality it covers. It gives you _nothing_ in return.

You might think you only watch very little and then only carefully selected programs of high cultural value. - But don't kid yourself. Even watching a little TV thoroughly undermines your ability to recognize the lines of action leading to inner expansion.

Get rid of these debilitating machines. You fully need to extract your consciousness from their paralyzing power if you seriously intend to discover any of the higher realities within yourself.

6 - Live vegetarian

Many experience more subtle insights once they completely switch to vegetarian food.

So - give it a try. Don't eat any kind of meat or fish for two solid months. You should feel the effect 4 to 6 weeks after the switch.

Then decide whether you prefer the clarity of mind, the lightness of your body and the easiness of comprehension you now experience to the fleeting taste of meat or fish - and make your decision permanent.

But - if you go for this test - become 100% vegetarian for this time. Don't break your intent even once or for any (social) reason during this period. Otherwise you might not feel any effect.

Water only boils at 100° Celsius, - below this temperature nothing will start. Do it wholeheartedly.

7 - Be courageous - don't fear

And finally - be courageous in your quest for higher stages of development. Fear is always only acquired. And most of the time it is entirely groundless.

Sure, - any conscious confrontation with situations whose outcome is uncertain and unforeseeable may cause initial fear or apprehension. Don't be afraid of this 'initial fear' itself. Don't permit fears to run your life.

You cannot escape fear by avoiding situations you believe will produce fear. This merely directs this negative emotion towards _other_ situations, persons or objects.

Courageously confront your fears, realize how unnecessary they are, and then be free of them.

Pericles - Athenian admiral and statesman (495-429 BC) successfully defended Athens against overwhelming outside aggression and brought about its highest bloom. He lived true to his words -

> *'Knoweth -*
> *the secret of happiness is freedom,*
> *but freedom's secret is courage.'*

Checklist for Real Growth

To cut out - copy - carry with you - realize

<u>General</u>

1 - recognize the many insights you already have

2 - always go for the highest choice

3 - really <u>do</u> what you intend to do

4 - make a list - arrange it - realize it - complete it

5 - stop watching TV

6 - live vegetarian

7 - be courageous - never fear

<u>Dissolve existing karma / prevent new karma</u>

- conduct your activities <u>consciously</u>
- be aware of your personal behavior
- consider the needs of others
- fundamentally rethink your situation
- prevent: - rage (anger) - arrogance (pride) - deceiving others (manipulation) - addiction (greed)
- dissolve: - prejudices, intolerance, laziness, skepticism etc.
- persevere when confronted with difficulties
- maintain equanimity
- re-evaluate deep-seated attitudes
- be open to new influences
- rise above personal boundaries: - think big, act big
- receive the love of others and give love
- direct thoughts and actions towards real freedom

- From 'HOW TO DISSOLVE KARMA' - KARMA - THE MECHANISM

Re-thinking Our Situation

- _Everything_ we confront in this world is transitory and subject to change.

- As long as we focus on limiting themes of life, we attract restrictions (karma) and experience them.

- The sequence of bodily existences we presently experience significantly restricts our potential abilities.

- _Only we_ cause all the situations and actions we experience.

- Our consciousness is fundamentally different from the non-living elements (matter, time, space etc.) that enable us to experience activity (karma) within this universe.

- Our present state of incarnation inhibits the perception of our real, majestic self.

- Our longing for limiting activities (karma) is the main cause for our bodily existence.

- We can stop this longing (for new karma).

- We can dissolve our prejudices, strong negative emotions, laziness, intolerance etc. (our existing karma).

- What do we expect of this universe?

- What is the purpose of reality - and do we live up to our part in it?

- How often do we gain access to effective methods that free us from all karmic restrictions?

- From 'HOW TO DISSOLVE KARMA' - KARMA - THE MECHANISM

Also by Hermann Kuhn

KARMA - THE MECHANISM

Create Your Own Fate

KARMA - THE MECHANISM is the counterpart to 'THE KEY TO THE CENTER OF THE UNIVERSE '. It introduces the third part of the ancient Indian manuscript *Tattvarthasutra* Hermann Kuhn discovered 1978.

KARMA - THE MECHANISM shows how to practically apply the mechanisms of expansion introduced in this book. It demonstrates how to discover far more exciting dimensions of our life. With many practical examples.

There is nothing mystic about karma !

It's a simple mechanism of daily life we are all unaware of, but which nevertheless influences us strongly.

Once we become aware how karma works, it opens new roads to success, happiness and an entirely new meaning to our life.

"An illuminating tool for personal and planetary transformation. The book offers us freedom from guilt, which does not exist in nature. A great work from a gifted teacher."
- LITTLE LIGHTNING FLOWER EAGLE, SHAMAN

ISBN 3-9806211-4-6   242 pages, paperback   US$ 15.00

CROSSWIND PUBLISHING
USA: P.O.Box 3312 • Incline Village • NV 89450
Phone   775 - 831 6687   Fax 775 - 831 9527

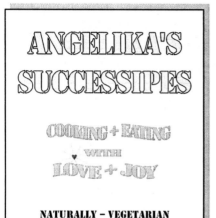

ANGELIKA'S
SUCCESSIPES

COOKING + EATING
♥ WITH
LOVE + JOY

NATURALLY – VEGETARIAN

Angelika Kuhn

CROSSWIND PUBLISHING

I'd love
to live
vegetarian
- but -
What shall I cook?

Simple, easy directions let you produce **delicious
international vegetarian dishes** in hardly any time.
- from breakfast to supper
- from hearty fare to the elegant dinner
- from food for journeys to your kids' favorite dishes

From France, Greece, Lebanon, Italy, Mexico, Germany,
India and - of course - from USA.

ANGELIKA'S SUCCESSIPES
COOKING + EATING   WITH   LOVE + JOY

Spiral-bound for practical use in the kitchen

ISBN 3-9806211-3-8   80 pages   US$ 5.00

CROSSWIND PUBLISHING